101 Activities for Happiness Workshops

Tom Bourner

Bridget Grenville-Cleave

Asher Rospigliosi

Info@happinessworkshops.org

Copyright ©2014 Tom Bourner, Bridget Grenville-Cleave, Asher Rospigliosi

The right of Tom Bourner, Bridget Grenville-Cleave and Asher Rospigliosi to be identified as the authors of this work has been asserted by them in accordance with the Copyright, Designs and Patents Act 1988.

First published 2014

The materials that appear in this book, other than those quoted from prior sources, may be reproduced for face-to-face education/training activities only. There is no requirement to obtain special permission for such uses.

This permission statement is limited to the reproduction of materials for face-to-face educational or training events. Systematic or large-scale reproduction or distribution, or transmission by other means, electronic, mechanical, recording or otherwise – or inclusion of items in publication for sale – may only be carried out with the prior written permission of the authors.

ISBN-13: 9781505219005
ISBN-10: 1505219000

This book is sold subject to the condition that it shall not, by way of trade or otherwise, be lent, resold, hired out, or otherwise circulated with the authors' prior consent in any form of binding or cover other than that in which it is published and without a similar condition including this condition being imposed upon the subsequent purchaser.

A catalogue record for this book is available from the British Library.

Cover design by Neil Ashley

Thanks To Our Generous Collaborators

This book is a collaborative project, like so many activities that lead to happiness. Besides the three named authors, we drew on the generosity of the international community of those who have an interest in happiness. Those listed below offered us ideas for activities which we felt free to draw on as we wrote the book. We are very grateful for their generosity and enthusiasm. We have asked each of them to share a website which they would want to bring to our readers' attention.

Our thanks to you all.

Tom, Bridget and Asher

Aaron Jarden	aaronjarden.com
Sarah Roberts	not-a-psychiatrist.blogspot.ca
Paul T.P. Wong	drpaulwong.com
Louisa Jewell	positivematters.com
Lisa Sansom	lvsconsulting.com
Linda Bolier	key-competence-happiness.eu
Light Box: The Happiness Project	wearelightbox.co.uk
Kristen Truempy	happyologist.co.uk
Kasley Killam	108days3habits.wordpress.com
Karen Skowron	homefree.blogs.com
Janet Peters	positivepsychology.org.nz
Ioanna N. Triperina	clevercareer.gr
Gitte Bjerre	enpp.eu
Frank Martela	waysofgoodliving.com
Dr Aymee Coget	happinessmakeover.com
Silvana Valentone	happy-cinco.tumblr.com

Tom Bourner
For Jill, Katie and Sally who contribute so much meaning to my life – and with thanks to Asher and Bridget whose particular strengths have made working on this book such an enjoyable experience.

Bridget Grenville-Cleave
I'd like to thank Neil and Hugo (my leading lights), Connie, Vanessa, Andy and Catherine for their support, inspiration and friendship along the way, and last but not least Tom and Asher for making it more fun less work.

Asher Rospigliosi
would like to thank his dad Guardino for encouragement, his wife Mitch for tolerance, his head of school, Aidan Berry, for generosity and his co-authors Tom and Bridget for their creativity and drive which has made this book happen.

We would also like to thank the many researchers and authors whose work we have referenced in this book. There is much frequently-used research employed in positive psychology and where we know the source we have been sure to acknowledge it. Our apologies to the originators of any material if we have overlooked them.

Preface

We wrote this because we'd like to live in a happier world and we believe that a book like this can make a contribution to that outcome. How? By supporting the development of more and better happiness workshops. The book is a resource for those who might consider running such a workshop to make it easier for them to do so. In that way, it can reduce the cost (in time and effort) of developing and putting on a happiness workshop.

Some happiness workshops already take place and we hope that the facilitators of such workshops will find activities in this book with which they are not yet familiar and which they choose to use. By giving them access to a wider range of activities we hope that the book will help them develop even better workshops.

It is also true that we have written this book to expand our own knowledge of workshop activities that can support more happiness and to expand our repertoire of happiness-enhancing activities.

The title of this book promises the reader 101 activities for happiness workshops. Actually, it contains 5 more than that, 106 activities. Why? Well, there are a lot of books with '101' in the title and we figure there has to be a reason for that ... even if it currently eludes us. Also, we thought you'd like it when you discovered you've got 5 bonus activities in addition to the number you thought you'd paid for. We think people like pleasant surprises so this might even increase your happiness.

In assembling these activities we've been mindful of the '*10 keys for happiness*' of the charity, *Action for Happiness* (AfH). There has been an explosion in evidence-based knowledge about happiness in recent years and the main rationale of AfH is to get that knowledge out of academic journals and into people's lives. AfH has classified most of this knowledge into what it calls '10 Keys for Happiness' as follows:

- *Giving i.e. doing things for others*
- *Relating, i.e. connecting with people*
- *Exercising, i.e. taking care of your body*
- *Appreciating, i.e. noticing and valuing the world around*
- *Trying out, i.e. continuing to learn new things*
- *Direction, i.e. having goals to look forward to*
- *Resilience, i.e. finding ways to bounce back*
- *Emotion, i.e. taking a positive approach*
- *Acceptance, i.e. being comfortable with who you are*
- *Meaning, i.e. being part of something bigger.*

We have tried to keep these keys in mind in producing this book. For this reason, the Table of Contents contains a column which lists the main happiness 'keys' which are addressed by each of the activities.

Table of Contents

	Page
Chapter 1: About This Book	1
Chapter 2: About Happiness	6
Chapter 3: About Workshops	10

Activities

No	Activity	Action for Happiness Key	Suitable for workshop start, middle or end	Other comments	Page
1	Extraordinary Achievements	Emotion, Direction, Relating	Start	Ice-breaker, pairs, groups	19
2	Happiness Journal	Emotion, Direction, Appreciating	Start	Individual, group, brainstorming	20
3	42 Varieties of Happiness	Trying out, Appreciating, Direction	Start	Group, brainstorming	21
4	Support Network	Relating, Direction	Start	Individual, pairs	22
5	Biography	Resilience, Acceptance, Meaning	Start	Individual, pairs	24
6	Strengths Brainstorm	Emotion, Acceptance	Start, middle	Individual, group, brainstorming	26
7	Appreciation	Appreciating	Start, middle	Individual, small groups	27
8	Have a Good Day	Emotion, Direction	Middle	Individual, pairs	29
9	Group Shoulder Massage	Giving, Appreciating, Emotion, Relating	Middle, end	Group	30
10	Giving Compliments	Giving, Appreciating, Emotion, Relating	Middle, end	Small groups	31
11	Past & Future Achievements	Emotion, Direction, Appreciating	Middle	Individual	33
12	Basic Relaxation	Emotion	Middle	Individual	34

No	Activity	Action for Happiness Key	Suitable for workshop start, middle or end	Other comments	Page
13	Purpose	Direction, Acceptance, Meaning	Middle	Individual, pairs	35
14	Loving-Kindness Mediation	Emotion, Acceptance, Relating	Middle, end	Individual	36
15	Sharing Good News	Relating, Emotion	Middle	Pairs	37
16	What Do You Notice?	Appreciating	Middle	Individual	38
17	Playful Haiku Writing	Appreciating, Emotion	Middle	Individual	40
18	Do a Secret Good Deed	Giving, Relating, Meaning, Emotion	Middle	Individual	41
19	Gratitude, Appreciation and Thankfulness	Appreciating, Giving, Relating, Meaning	Middle, end	Individual	42
20	Portraits	Emotion, Relating	Middle	Pairs	43
21	Inspiration	Relating, Appreciating	Start, middle	Individual, pairs	44
22	Tributes	Meaning, Direction	Middle	Individual	45
23	Rediscovering Happiness	Trying Out, Direction	Start	Individual, pairs	46
24	Happy Questions	Emotion, Trying Out, Direction	Start, middle	Pairs	48
25	Keeping a Happiness Log	Meaning, Appreciating, Direction	Start	Individual	50
26	Happiness Goals	Direction	End	Individual	52
27	Measure Your Happiness	Trying Out, Appreciating, Direction	Start, middle	Individual	53
28	Micro Activities	Trying Out, Direction	Start, middle	Individual	56
29	What's Going Right?	Emotion, Appreciating	Start, middle	Individual, pairs	57
30	Savour the Moment	Emotion, Appreciating	End	Individual	58
31	Appreciation & Gratitude for this Day	Appreciating	Middle	Individual	59
32	Optimism – Best Possible Self	Emotion, Direction, Appreciating	Middle, end	Individual	61

No	Activity	Action for Happiness Key	Suitable for workshop start, middle or end	Other comments	Page
33	Music Playlists	Emotion, Appreciating, Meaning	Middle	Group, brainstorming	63
34	Chucklebelly	Emotion	Middle	Group	64
35	Relaxation; Progressive Muscle Relaxation	Emotion, Appreciating	Middle	Individual	65
36	Relaxation – Basic Visualisation	Emotion	Middle	Individual	67
37	Raisin Meditation	Appreciating	Middle	Individual	68
38	Smiles Cocktail Party	Emotion, Relating	Middle	Pairs, small groups	70
39	Faking It 1 – Method Acting	Emotion, Trying Out, Relating	Middle	Pairs, small groups	71
40	Faking It 2 – Postures	Emotion, Trying Out, Relating	Middle	Individual	72
41	Some Facts About Happiness	Trying Out	Start, middle	Individual, pairs	73
42	Reasons to be Happy	Trying Out, Direction	Start, middle	Individual, pairs	76
43	Rip it Up!	Trying Out, Direction	Middle	Individual, groups	80
44	Pub Quiz on Happiness	Appreciating, Trying Out	Start, middle	Small groups	81
45	Best Possible Past Life	Resilience	Middle	Individual, pairs	88
46	Blissful Guided Imagery	Emotion	Middle, end	Individual	89
47	Integrated Meditation	Emotion	End	Individual	92
48	Connections and Friendship	Relating, Trying Out	Middle, end	Individual, pairs	93
49	One Small Piece of Chocolate	Emotion, Relating	Middle, end	Pairs	95
50	Vocational Mapping	Trying Out, Direction	Middle	Individual	96
51	Signature Strengths	Trying Out, Direction	Middle, end	Individual, pairs	98
52	Giving Positive Feedback on Strengths	Giving, Relating, Emotion	Middle	Individual	99

No	Activity	Action for Happiness Key	Suitable for workshop start, middle or end	Other comments	Page
53	Questions for Happiness	Emotion	Start, middle	Individual, pairs	101
54	Quotes about Happiness	Trying Out	Middle	Individual, pairs	103
55	Inner Sage	Trying Out, Direction, Meaning	Middle	Individual	105
56	Finding Happiness Outside of the Comfort Zone	Trying Out	Start	Individual	107
57	Happiness Quotations	Emotion, Meaning	Middle	Individual	108
58	Tokens of Appreciation	Giving, Appreciating, Relating	Middle	Individual	109
59	Strengths Date	Giving, Emotion, Relating	Middle	Individual, pairs	110
60	Good News Stories	Emotion, Appreciating	Middle	Small groups	111
61	Strengths Notes	Emotion, Relating, Giving, Appreciating	Middle	Individual	112
62	Secret Notes	Emotion, Relating, Giving, Appreciating	Middle, end	Individual	113
63	Nature's Treasures	Appreciating, Emotion, Meaning	Middle	Individual	114
64	Life through a Lens	Trying out, Resilience, Acceptance, Meaning	Start, middle	Individual	116
65	If/Then Intentions	Trying out, Direction	End	Individual	117
66	Happiness Playlist	Emotion, Acceptance, Direction	Middle, end	Individual	118
67	Let it Flow!	Trying out, Direction, Emotion	Middle	Individual, pairs	119
68	Wheel of Well-being	Trying out, Direction, Emotion	Start, middle	Individual	121
69	Mental Time Travelling	Emotion, Relating, Appreciating	Middle	Individual, pairs	123
70	Savouring	Emotion, Appreciating	Middle, end	Individual	124
71	Forgiveness Letter	Trying Out, Emotion, Resilience	Middle	Individual	126
72	How Flexible is Your Thinking?	Trying out, Resilience	Middle	Small groups	127
73	Counting Kindnesses	Appreciating, Emotion	Middle	Individual	129

No	Activity	Action for Happiness Key	Suitable for workshop start, middle or end	Other comments	Page
74	Treasure Chest	Emotion	Middle, end	Individual	130
75	Humour Diary	Emotion, Appreciating	Middle	Individual	131
76	Disputing Negative Thoughts	Resilience, Trying out, Emotion	Middle	Individual	132
77	Resilience Timeline	Resilience, Trying out, Acceptance	Middle	Individual	135
78	Appreciating Our Relationships	Relating, Emotion, Trying out, Meaning	Middle	Pairs	136
79	Strengths Spotting	Emotion, Trying out, Acceptance, Relating	Middle	Pairs	137
80	Family Strengths Tree	Relating, Emotion, Trying out	Middle	Individual	138
81	Resilience Hero	Resilience, Trying out, Acceptance, Emotion, Meaning	Middle	Individual	139
82	Open Doors	Resilience, Trying out, Emotion, Appreciating, Meaning	Middle	Pairs	140
83	Vital Friends	Relating, Trying out	Middle	Individual	141
84	Aims and Guidelines	Direction, Trying out	Start	Individual	142
85	Just Walking	Relating, Trying out, Emotion, Exercise	Middle	Individual, pairs	144
86	Human Bingo	Emotion, Relating	Start	Individual, groups	146
87	People Hunting	Emotion, Relating	Start	Individual, small groups	148
88	A Few Things about Me	Emotion, Acceptance, Relating, Direction	Start	Individual, small groups	152
89	Letter to Self	Direction, Trying out	End	Individual	154
90	Stop, Start and Continue	Direction, Trying out	End	Individual	155
91	Simple Feedback Form	Giving, Appreciating	End	Individual	157
92	Stop and Notice	Trying out, Direction	Middle	Small groups	159
93	Closing Round – 3 Options	Emotion, Direction, Appreciating	End	Individual	160

No	Activity	Action for Happiness Key	Suitable for workshop start, middle or end	Other comments	Page
94	Dreams	Meaning, Direction	End	Individual, pairs	162
95	Telling Stories	Relating, Emotion, Trying out, Direction	Middle	Pairs	164
96	Happiness Advantage	Exercise, Giving, Relating, Appreciating	Middle	Pairs	165
97	Appreciating the Big Things	Meaning, Appreciating, Trying out, Acceptance	Middle	Individual	166
98	Trying something else	Trying out, Direction	Middle	Threes	167
99	New Views	Trying out, Relating, Acceptance	Middle	Small groups	168
100	Some Things I Like	Acceptance, Emotion	Middle	Pairs	170
101	Simple Massage	Giving, Relating, Emotion	Middle	Pairs	171
102	Polishing Diamonds	Emotion, Appreciating, Acceptance, Meaning	Middle	Individual	173
103	Sharing Happiness	Relating, Trying out, Direction	Middle	Pairs, threes	175
104	Whose Strengths?	Relating, Giving, Appreciating, Acceptance	Middle	Individual, group	176
105	What Strengths?	Relating, Giving, Appreciating, Acceptance	Middle	Individual, small groups	178
106	Parting Gifts	Relating, Giving, Emotion, Acceptance	End	Individual, small groups	179

Appendix 1: Some Flexible Workshop Processes — 180

Appendix 2: Outline Plan for a Happiness Workshop — 186

Appendix 3: Sample Programme Design for a Happiness Workshop — 187

Where to Find Out More about Happiness and Positive Psychology — 189

Useful Websites — 190

References — 193

About the Authors — 196

Chapter 1: About This Book

What is this book about?

This book is about activities that can be included in a happiness workshop. Over the last couple of decades our knowledge of how to increase sustainable happiness has been accumulating rapidly. The book contains activities intended to convey some of that knowledge in ways that will help workshop participants apply it within their own lives. It does not include activities based on prescriptions for increasing happiness arising solely from speculation, received wisdom or personal experience.

We believe that the aims of a happiness workshop should include: (1) to convey some of the new knowledge about how to realise more sustainable happiness, (2) to develop the commitment of participants to take actions that will raise the likelihood of their living happier lives and (3) to directly enhance their positive feelings so that they leave the workshop feeling happier than when they arrived. These aims have guided our selection of activities for this book. Some of the activities focus on one of those aims, some on two of them and some on all three. When considering activities to include in this book we omitted any that did not contribute to at least one of those aims.

Another criterion we used for deciding whether to include an activity was whether it would involve some active learning. Simply listening to a talk on a happiness-related topic involves participants only as passive recipients of knowledge so, for the most part, we rejected ideas with that form. This is a book of workshop activities so naturally we have exercised a preference for learning processes that are active.

The activities in the book are evidence-based, i.e. they are underpinned by empirical research. However, although we've learned a great deal from science in recent years about what contributes to happier lives there remains the problem of how to apply that knowledge and that is more of an art. So the activities themselves, unlike the knowledge that underpins them, are based on personal experience, shared experience of others in the field of positive psychology and professional judgement about what works well in a workshop setting.

One important consequence of the explosion of knowledge about happiness over the last 2 decades has been a very large escalation in the number of books published that seek to popularise the results of research on happiness. Many of these have been written by professors of psychology at prestigious universities. At the end of this book we've provided details of some of these books.

Books can only go so far, however, as increasing happiness needs more than intellectual assent to new knowledge; it requires action to implement that knowledge and changes in behaviours. This is one reason for disillusion with self-help books; they often contain much sensible advice but intellectual assent to such advice is not much help if habits and behaviours remain unchanged.

We can't emphasise this enough. Just learning about happiness will not necessarily make you happier. It is only when your new knowledge impacts on your actions and your behaviours that you can expect to enjoy a significant and sustained increase in your happiness. There is an old saying that 'if you always do what you've always done, then you'll always get what you've always got'. And this applies equally to happiness.

Reading about good nutrition will not of itself improve your health or reduce your weight. Reading about the result of studies on the benefits of health will not, per se, make you fitter. Likewise, reading about the findings of studies on the sources and causes of happiness will not of itself make you happier if you don't actually do something as a result.

This is where happiness workshops come in. Books about happiness engage mostly the intellect whereas workshops about happiness can also engage the emotions and actions. This is why they can be powerful in motivating behavioural change and producing new actions, which means it is more likely that workshop participants will try out different behaviours after the workshop. And, of course, workshops can contain activities which enable participants to actually try out different behaviours within the workshop where they feel supported.

This rationale for workshops helped us decide which activities to include in the book. It also provides a clue to the sort of activities to include in a happiness workshop: (1) activities that convey knowledge, (2) activities that engage the emotions and (3) activities that lead to action and new behaviours.

Who is the book intended for?

In producing this book we had in mind people who want to develop and run workshops that will contribute to a happier world. We feel it will also be particularly valuable to:

- People who already run happiness workshops and are on the look-out for additional ideas to use or adapt.
- People who run workshops in other fields and who would like to extend their repertoire to include happiness workshops.
- People who run workshops in other fields and who would like to add the occasional happiness activity to their existing workshop content in order to boost the mood of participants
- People who facilitate other sorts of events, such as yoga, exercise classes and other complementary therapies and who would like to develop happiness workshops.
- People who work as coaches on a one-to-one basis and would now like to extend their practice to running workshops or who would like to include the occasional happiness activity within their current practice to boost the mood of their coaching clients.
- Teachers of positive psychology who will find some of the activities directly applicable to their classes.

Having said that, the best person to decide if this book is likely to be of value to you is yourself. We suggest you browse the contents of this book and decide how the ideas and activities in it can be helpful to you personally.

For the most part, such happiness workshops as currently exist are 'open' workshops in the sense that they are open to anyone. There are two specific areas where we would like to see more happiness workshops developed: schools and organisations that employ people.

What is the point of school? We believe it is to prepare children for life after school. This, of course, goes much further than preparing children for work after school. Work is part of life, but it is only part. Presumably we want our children to live long happy lives. How well does school prepare them for long happy lives? Ironically it doesn't seem to be easy for schools to find space in the curriculum to prepare children for happy lives. One solution is to embed happiness workshops into the school-year. The activities in this book will facilitate the development of such workshops.

The other area with considerable potential for the development of happiness workshops is the corporate sector or, more accurately, all organisations that employ people, including those in the public sector and the not-for-profit sector. Why would organisations want to put on such workshops? There are at least three reasons. First, there is much evidence that happy employees are more productive. Second, a one-day happiness workshop could be a great reward for excellent results. Third, a happiness workshop would be good for team-building purposes.

In addition, groups of people are now coming together to facilitate their own happiness. For example, *Action for Happiness* encourages the establishment of local groups to raise happiness and awareness of happiness. Such groups could choose to work through many of the activities in this book.

Who is this book *not* for? It is not for people who want a ready-made happiness workshop. The book contains the ingredients, but you need to combine them and 'cook' them yourself. And the book is not for people who want an account of the latest research on happiness. There are plenty of books that report recent knowledge gained about happiness. At the end of this book we give details of some of them.

What <u>kind</u> of book is this?

This book is intended to be a general resource for people who run, or wish to run, workshops intended to raise the sustainable happiness of participants. If that applies to you then we think you will find this book helpful and interesting. It contains a range of practical ideas and activities for running such workshops.

In writing this book we have been able to share ideas gained from the evidence-based literature on happiness, our own experience, the web and the experience of others.

What's special about it?

In this book we've assembled a large range of ideas and activities to choose from as you set about developing a happiness workshop or reviewing one that you already run. All the activities are based on evidence about what makes for happier lives. We chose not to include much discussion of the theory behind each activity but to focus on the processes themselves. One reason is that there are many other books that discuss the theory and evidence that supports the new knowledge about happiness. This book focuses on practices that get some of that new knowledge out of those texts and into people's lives.

How to use this book

This book contains over one hundred activities that can be used as part of a happiness workshop. Many could be used by happiness groups as regular or occasional activities. And many could also be used as exercises on courses of positive psychology, some at school level and others at university level.

Clearly this is not a book to be read from cover to cover. It is a resource book, a book to *do* rather than read. Having said that, it might make sense to read the introductory chapters first to clarify where we are coming from, and that could affect how (when, where and with whom) you use the activities.

The introductory chapters are likely to be most valuable for those with least experience of facilitating happiness workshops or indeed facilitating workshops generally.

Facilitation is a very personal and individual thing and what works best for one person does not suit the facilitation style of others. We recommend that you use the activities for inspiration rather than following them slavishly. So please feel free to take the core idea in an activity and then apply your own knowledge, experience and intuition. Feel free to modify it in any way(s) that you think will work best for you and your own facilitation style in the particular context in which you wish to use it.

Beyond that, there are a whole range of ways to use this book and here are a few:

Edit, amend and add to the activities: You can use this book as a starting point and a source of inspiration to develop your own ideas. Try them out your own way and certainly don't feel you have to follow each activity to the letter.

Sample the activities: This is a book to be dipped into rather than read from start to finish. So scan it for ideas that are most likely to get the results you want.

Write on this book: You can scribble in the margins and add your own comments and notes. To help you do this, we've produced a book with ample white space for you to write on.

Create your own index: You can stick 'Post-it' notes to the margins of this book to mark the activities you are using for a particular workshop. This will make an index for the activities for that particular workshop.

Reorder this book: If you would like the contents of the book in a different order then cut out the pages – a guillotine will be easiest but you can also do it with scissors or a sharp knife – and put the pages into a ring binder in the sequence that you'd prefer. This is a resource book so just use the pages with the resources that are most relevant to you and the aims of your particular workshop.

Let participants know about this book: Our aim is to encourage the development of happiness workshops and if you share our aim then share the book. Let the participants know where you got the activities so they can do the same.

Distribute copies of the book: You might want to do this, for example, if you run a workshop on running happiness workshops.

Use the book to reflect on the experience of running the workshop: You can use the book to review and reflect afterwards on how your workshop went. Use some of the white space in the book to note things you tried that worked out particularly well as well as for things you'd do differently next time.

What is the philosophy of this book?

This book reflects, of course, the philosophies of its authors. In particular, it reflects what is shared in our respective beliefs about happiness. This has several strands. First, is a commitment to evidence-based knowledge about happiness. We are interested in all ideas about how to increase happiness, but we're *most* interested in evidence-based ideas. By evidence-based we mean based on empirical evidence. Knowledge gained from scientific study carries most weight with us. That's why the activities we've included in this book are underpinned by such knowledge. This is why, for example, it includes activities to help people express appreciation and gratitude, because systematic scientific studies support this as a path to more happiness.

A second strand is the relationship between happiness and positive psychology which is the academic field within which most studies of happiness are located. Positive psychology is a relatively new field of academic enquiry. Martin Seligman and Mihaly Csikszentmihalyi are usually credited as its founders and Seligman's address as president-elect of the prestigious American Psychological Association in 1998 as the time of its birth. Four years later, 2002, Seligman published a book titled 'Authentic Happiness' which was a landmark publication for the new discipline. And 9 years later, in 2011, he recanted his earlier advocacy of happiness as the over-arching goal in favour of a broader conception of 'flourishing'.

This contains five elements which can be summarised in the acronym, PERMA: (1) Positive Emotions, (2) Engagement, (3) Relationships, (3) Meaning and (5) Accomplishment. According to Seligman, these are all ends that humans pursue for themselves and they are independent of each other.

We don't quite buy into this perspective, rather we see each of those five elements as ingredients that contribute to happiness. That is why we have included activities in this book aimed at increasing each of these elements in the lives of workshop participants. More generally, so-called positive psychology 'interventions' have provided the basis of a significant proportion of the activities in this book.

One difficulty with the concept of happiness is that it is not a very well-defined term. Serene contentment and wild elation are very different but they can both be recognised as states of happiness. There is a wide range of varieties of happiness, including for example: delight, pride, love, jubilation, sensual pleasure, personal growth, spiritual elevation and intellectual satisfaction. This suggests that there are many different sources of happiness and many different paths to happiness.

Positive psychology makes a clear distinction between hedonic happiness and eudaimonic happiness. Hedonic happiness is happiness associated with the senses and pleasure. Eudaimonic happiness is the happiness of a life well-lived and human potential realised.

In this book we're interested in both forms of happiness. We have included activities that will convey knowledge (often experientially) about how to live lives of greater satisfaction and we've included activities that are mood-enhancing. We believe that when a person completes a happiness workshop they should learn how to live a life about which they can express more satisfaction and we believe also that when they leave a happiness workshop they should be in a better mood than when they started it. In other words, we believe that the two types of happiness are conceptually distinct but they are not incompatible and they are certainly not mutually exclusive.

Chapter 2: About Happiness

Why happiness? Why positive psychology? Why now?

Human beings have probably been interested in living happier lives for as long as there have been human beings. And a great deal has been written about happiness over the last few thousand years. Most of what has been written about it over that period has been based on personal experience, introspection or received wisdom. The problem with personal experience as a source of knowledge about happiness is that different people have different experiences and this can lead to different, sometimes conflicting, advice for living happier lives. That is also the trouble with introspection as a source of knowledge. Moreover, recent research (such as Wilson and Gilbert, 2005) on affective forecasting has cast doubt on the value of introspection as a source of knowledge about happiness; it shows that we are pretty poor at forecasting and even remembering what makes us happy.

Much of the received wisdom about happiness has come from philosophical, religious or spiritual sources. Jonathan Haidt's book '*The Happiness Hypothesis: Putting Ancient Wisdom to the Test of Modern Science*' does exactly what its title says, with the result that some of that 'wisdom' has been supported by scientific study of happiness and some has been challenged.

There was a time, particularly the first three-quarters of the 20th century, when science steered clear of happiness as a field of study. It was regarded as too subjective to permit serious scientific enquiry. In recent decades, however, the development of brain imaging techniques and technology has given psychologists much more confidence in our ability to measure positive emotions. And the emergence of positive psychology as part of mainstream psychology in the late 1990s has lead to a huge increase in the number of researchers and other academics studying happiness as a significant part of positive psychology. The result has been an explosion in evidence-based knowledge about happiness.

This increase in our knowledge about happiness has coincided with an escalation of interest in happiness and its causes. It has become apparent that there are limits to the power of increasing national income to raise the level of happiness in a country. The world's richest countries have more than doubled their material standard of living in the last 50 years but there has been no significant rise in recorded happiness in these countries (Layard, 2011, Ch. 3). Consequently, many governments across the world, including the UK, have been exploring the development of National Wellbeing Accounts as an alternative or as a complement to National Income Accounts.

In other words, the last two decades has seen an increase in the supply of knowledge about happiness as well as an increase in the demand for knowledge about happiness. The aim of this chapter is therefore to dispel some of the myths about happiness, to highlight some of the most important research findings on happiness and to outline other sources of information about happiness if you want to find out more.

Feeling good, functioning well and flourishing

Even though some of the top universities across the world (Harvard, University of Pennsylvania, University of Sydney, University of Glasgow to name but a few) offer degrees and other courses in positive psychology, and even though countless clinically-trained and professionally-accredited psychologists work in the field, one of the most common criticisms we hear is that happiness is just too frivolous a topic to be worth taking seriously.

When we tell people that we run happiness workshops we sometimes get raised eyebrows. They say things like 'but we all know what happiness means, don't we?' and 'isn't happiness just about feeling good?' Having studied the topic and worked in this field for many years as consultants, coaches, lecturers and authors, we know that it's not as simple as that. Nevertheless, misconceptions about the simple nature of happiness continue.

One reason for this is the word itself, and its popular connotations. It's true that 'happiness' is most often associated with simply feeling good. It brings to mind words and phrases like 'having fun', 'enjoyment', 'pleasure' and 'having a laugh'. It's light-hearted, carefree and perhaps even a bit flippant. This form of happiness is what positive psychologists often refer to as hedonic well-being. On the other side of the coin we have eudaimonic well-being, the more serious cousin of hedonic well-being. Eudaimonic approaches include personal growth, self-realisation, autonomy, self-acceptance, and meaning and purpose; in other words they refer not to feeling good, per se, but to functioning well.

In the early days of positive psychology it was suggested that eudaimonic approaches to happiness were more objective and morally-valid and therefore more worthwhile than hedonic approaches, however there now appears to be a general consensus that both are desirable, since combined they can lead to a state of flourishing.

Feeling good is a vital part of enduring happiness

It's worth stressing that although we commonly refer to 'the pursuit of happiness' as if there is one magic key which opens all the doors, there are actually many different routes. As mentioned in the previous chapter, Seligman's PERMA model (Seligman, 2011) incorporates five different pathways (positive emotion, engagement, relationships, meaning and accomplishment). These five elements were chosen on the basis that they all contribute to our well-being and they are things that people pursue for its own sake (not merely to get any of the other elements) and because they can be defined and measured independently. Scientific research suggests that certain activities, such as taking regular physical exercise, playing to your strengths, disputing negative thoughts, expressing gratitude and practising mindfulness, are pretty fool-proof ways to boost your mood, overcome stress and develop resilience. Even better is that these activities needn't require a huge investment in time, and before long they can become part of your daily routine, your normal way of living and being.

New studies are being carried out all the time to test the efficacy of certain happiness-inducing activities in certain conditions. Some of them have even turned our preconceived ideas about happiness upside down. For example, Barbara Fredrickson's research (Frederickson, 2009) suggests that contrary to popular opinion positive emotions aren't only about feeling good; they also do us good in a number of important ways:

- They broaden the way we think and encourage us to be more open-minded and adopt new behaviours.

- They build additional personal resources such as optimism, resilience and social bonds over the longer term.

- They undo the physiological effects (such as raised blood pressure and heart rate) of experiencing negative emotions such as anger, anxiety and fear.

Studies reveal that positive emotions don't last very long compared to negative ones; they tend to be quite fleeting. Positive psychology studies also show that we adapt pretty quickly to most positive events and experiences, returning to a relatively stable level of happiness (our 'happiness set-point') after the event or experience has finished. Think about the last time you went shopping and treated yourself to a new pair of shoes or the latest gadget and you'll know what we're getting at. The pleasure you felt from that purchase probably lasted a few days at most. Then you're pretty much back where you started.

These two conclusions suggest that finding ways to experience more frequent 'low level' positive emotions such as contentment, gratitude and interest is likely to be a more effective route to longer-lasting happiness than waiting for the occasional experience of intense positive emotions like ecstasy, bliss and elation. Giving up a reliance on 'retail therapy' to boost your mood will also help your pocket!

The Importance of Emotions and Engagement

At the same time, we don't want to fall into the trap of thinking that positive emotions are always good and negative emotions are always bad. This is simply not the case. Nor is it true that emotions are just reactions to events and experiences. Yes if you were to win an award you would probably feel very proud and if someone threatened you, you would probably feel anxious. But there's more to it than that.

All emotions provide useful information - they help us make decisions, help other people understand us, help us understand ourselves and other people, they motivate us to take action and ultimately help us survive and thrive. Positive psychology isn't about denying the negative, or about ridding ourselves of every negative emotion. Negative emotions have their place. All of us at some point in our lives will have to deal with adverse events or experiences. Where positive psychology comes in is in studying how to build resilience, how to reduce the impact of negative emotions and how to cope in effective and sustainable ways, which mean that we recover our equilibrium more quickly.

We also know that positive and negative emotions are not merely opposites, which means that the absence of negative emotions does not automatically mean that someone is happy. In order to be happy we need to do more than simply overcome negative emotions.

Scientific research also suggests that 'flow' (sometimes referred to as engagement, that is, the experience of being so fully absorbed in what you're doing that time passes without you noticing, followed by a feeling of well-being) can be achieved by participating in all sorts of negative behaviours. So it's perfectly possible that a shoplifter could experience flow whilst s/he's stealing goods from a shop.

We mention these points to highlight the complexity of happiness. We want to challenge the tendency to dismiss happiness as flippant, frivolous or facile or as something straightforward and easy to achieve. It's unlikely that happiness will just land in your lap. There are many evidence-based ways to increase happiness and the one thing they all have in common is that they require effort. You have to do something. As Chris Peterson once said, happiness is not for sissies.

Ten important findings about happiness

- The way we respond to people's good news is even more important than how we respond to their bad news. Responding in an 'active and constructive' style helps the other person to capitalise on their positive emotions, makes them feel validated and cared for, and ultimately helps build stronger relationships.
- Using your strengths in new ways has been shown to increase well-being and reduce depressive symptoms over the longer term.
- Expressing gratitude (for example, writing about three good things once a week) helps to overcome the inbuilt negativity bias and create an orientation towards the positive.
- Finding ways to experience more frequent positive emotions and enhancing our ability to notice positive emotions (as well as reducing our experience of negative emotions) is important not just

for feeling good. We know that positive emotions help us function well i.e. they are linked to a great many other benefits (such as creativity, sociability and better physical health).
- Experiencing positive emotions helps us 'see the bigger picture' and makes us more open-minded towards and tolerant of other people.
- Resilience is a skill that can be learnt, which means that even if you don't feel naturally resilient, you can learn how to overcome negative thoughts and bounce back from adversity, disappointments and set-backs more readily.
- Pretty much anything, apart from sleeping, can be done mindfully - eating, walking, sitting, brushing your hair or your teeth, dressing/undressing, driving, polishing your shoes, chopping vegetables, washing up and, of course, breathing. This is great news as it provides so many more opportunities to practice the skills of focused attention.
- Expressing gratitude is so important that it has been called a meta-strategy for achieving happiness (Lyubomirsky, 2008). It works in part by helping turn your attention to what is going well rather than what isn't. Fortunately there are numerous ways to do it, including writing a gratitude diary or a thank-you letter or card to someone who has helped you, finding three good things in your life, appreciating the beauty of the world around you, focussing on what went well today rather than what didn't and being thankful for the food on your plate. You can even express gratitude that water runs out of the tap when you turn it on, as does one of our colleagues who works for a water charity. And remember to tell the people around you (family, friends, colleagues, neighbours) why you appreciate them – it will help them feel good too.
- Smiling predicts a longer life, by between 5 and 8 years. Of course, this doesn't mean that if you go round grinning inanely that you'll suddenly live longer. It suggests that doing the sorts of things that produce lasting happiness (and which bring a genuine smile to your face) are really beneficial in terms of longevity. Plus you'll have a better time, and so will the people around you who have to look at you!
- Having good quality relationships is one of the strongest predictors of happiness. In research the only significant difference between the top 10% of happiest people and everyone else was their relationships. Additionally people who have stronger relationships (quantitatively and qualitatively) have a 50% increased likelihood of survival, in other words, a longer life. So, not only are our personal relationships important for happiness, they are also important for longevity. Quite amazing, don't you think?

Chapter 3: About Workshops

Designing and facilitating happiness workshops

We've written this chapter mainly for the benefit of less experienced workshop facilitators. If you are an experienced facilitator you'll probably want to skip over it. On the other hand, you might be curious and want to compare our thoughts on happiness workshops and how to run them with your own.

What is a workshop?

What exactly is a workshop? We believe that a workshop has four significant ingredients:

1. *Sharing experience* In a workshop, participants learn from the experience of each other. The participants are a resource in a workshop as is their past and current experience. So the participants can expect to learn from each other in a workshop as well as from the workshop leader. Participants contribute in a workshop; it is an event in which the participants give as well as receive.
2. *Active learning* In workshops the participants do things; they don't just sit and listen and make notes.
3. *Variety* A good workshop will have a mixture of processes and a variety of activities. In this book we have assembled ideas for activities to use in your happiness workshops to gain and hold the attention of the participants and maintain their interest.
4. *Whole person* A good workshop will involve participants in thinking, doing and feeling. In other words, it will engage their intellects, their actions and their emotions.

Happiness workshops are a more effective way of initiating changes in behaviours than just reading about what affects happiness. This is partly because there is often an emotional content to workshop activities and emotion is an important element in prompting action (Damasio, 1994), it's partly because workshop participants can practice new behaviours (e.g. through activities such as role-playing) and it's partly because workshops provide a social context for learning new behaviours. Also, there is an experiential aspect to learning in workshops that is absent in learning propositional knowledge from books and other text-based sources.

Developing a workshop

A good place to start developing a workshop is by imagining what you want it to be like. If you imagine running a really successful workshop you can form a vision of the best possible outcome for your workshop. What does 'successful' mean to you in this context? Lots of people? Participants who are delighted that they came? People who are confident they will live happier lives as a result? Smiling, happy faces of people leaving the workshop and chattering enthusiastically about the experience? Getting really clear about the outcomes you want in terms of a compelling vision will help you plan your workshop and also motivate you, which is especially important if you encounter obstacles along the way.

The next first step is to turn that motivating vision into something more concrete and to clarify your ideas about the workshop. Answering the following questions can be helpful is doing this:
    1. What is the rationale for this workshop?
    2. What are your aims for this workshop?

3. What do you see as the main learning outcomes?
4. What is the main content of the workshop?
5. What sort of processes will be used?

With answers to these questions you'll be in a good position to produce a broad outline for your workshop. Appendix 2 provides an example.

Next comes the questions of 'who' and 'where'? You need to ask yourself who do you want to attract and who is likely to turn up as participants? The answer to the 'who?' question is likely to be related to the answer to the 'where?' question. For example, if you are running the workshop for an organisation (e.g. a company or a school) then that will largely determine the answer to the 'who' question. The sort of workshop you plan for a group of university staff is likely to be significantly different to one you run at a local complementary health centre.

Once you have a better idea of who the participants will be and where the workshop will take place you'll be in a better position to do some more detailed planning. You'll be able to develop your outline plan into a more detailed programme. Moreover, you'll also be in a position to produce it from the perspective of the potential participants. So, for example, instead of recording just your own objectives you'll now be able to produce learning outcomes that you feel will appeal to prospective participants.

A typical set of objectives could be phrased along the following lines:

The objective of this workshop is to give you the opportunity to:
  1. acquire some evidence-based knowledge about how to live happier lives
  2. explore ways of applying that knowledge to your own life
  3. discover some ideas about how to share more happiness with those around you, including those people you care most about
  4. have an enjoyable and happy overall experience at the workshop
  5. meet other people with an interest in living happier lives and sharing that happiness with others.

Once you're clear about your aims for the workshop and the learning outcomes, you'll be more able to consider how to realise those aims and outcomes by choosing activities for your workshop. That's where this book comes in.

In choosing workshop activities it is important to get the attention of participants at the outset. If you don't have their attention then really you don't have anything to work with. That's why we've included activities like 'Extraordinary Achievements', because we know that it captures the attention of participants.

When choosing a variety of activities for your workshop it can be helpful to consider the participants' experience in terms of body, mind and emotions. Is there sufficient variation in what you're asking them to do (body), what you're asking them to think (mind) and what you're asking them to feel (emotions)? The greater the variety you can introduce in each of these dimensions the more likely it will be that you workshop will offer a rich experience that participants will find engaging and memorable.

Stages of a happiness workshop

The most obvious stages are the early stage, the middle stage and the last stage, in other words, getting going, getting on with it and getting ready to go. But there are two other stages to consider: before and after.

Before the workshop

Check out the venue in advance:

- *Temperature*. Is your room too cold or too hot? You may wish to check before you start the workshop that you can control the temperature of the workshop room.
- *Thirst*. Are coffee, tea, fruit juice and/or water available? If not, you probably need to provide it.
- *Comfort breaks*. It can be difficult to concentrate when what you really want right now is a pee. Plenty of comfort breaks is one solution. Another is an explicit ground-rule at the outset that anyone can take a comfort break at any time without a 'by-your-leave'.
- *Noise*. Will the traffic outside make it difficult for some people to hear?
- *Light*. Is your room gloomy? Lights that are too bright can also be a distraction. Are any of the lights in the room flickering, because this can be annoying.
- *Ventilation*. Is the room too stuffy? Can you open a window without letting in too much traffic noise? Is it worth opening all the windows for a time before the workshop to freshen the air? Is it worth opening all the windows during breaks to change the air?

Think about the range of activities you have planned and then make provision for them in terms of the room layout you use – this might include, for example, sitting, writing, moving into smaller groups, milling around, working with a partner etc.

Getting going – the first part

You only get one chance to make a good first impression. When participants start arriving make sure they know where to go and where the toilets are. Consider putting signs up around the building.

When you start the workshop welcome the participants and then introduce yourself. How you do this will help set the tone for the workshop because one of the things you'll be doing, as a workshop facilitator, is modelling behaviour. It can be easier if the participants have already seen a brief CV for you, e.g. as an element in your flier for the workshop. Then you can introduce yourself by disclosing a few personal details about yourself such as your likes and dislikes or key beliefs and values.

Help participants to get to know each other or at least a few of the other participants. New groups can feel a bit threatening so giving participants an opportunity to learn a little more about who the other participants are helps them refocus their attention to the main business of this workshop: living happier lives and sharing that happiness. We have included a few activities in this book to help participants get to know each other.

Find out exactly what your participants want out of this workshop. This may not be entirely what you had planned or may be a particular emphasis on something or some things within the broad theme of your workshop. With this information you can often steer the activities towards what the participants particularly want as well as achieving your own objectives for the workshop. As a result, you will have a more successful workshop and happier participants. Again, we have included a couple of activities to help surface the particular wants of participants.

Now the participants know a bit more about you and what you stand for, feel welcomed into this group and have had an opportunity to express what they most want from the workshop, you'll be in a good position to start realising the aims of the workshop.

Getting on with it – the middle part

Hopefully, you will have put together a workshop which contains the essential ingredients of an effective workshop:
1. Plenty of opportunities for participants to share experience – where they can use each other's experience, knowledge and expertise as a resource.
2. Active learning - where they can do things.
3. Variety of processes – to capture and hold their attention.
4. Activities that engage participants' intellects, actions and emotions.

Your role in the workshop is now to facilitate the process and help participants get the most learning from their experience at the workshop. What sort of things will this involve? Probably most of the following at one time or another:

- Developing a climate that helps participants to learn
- Listening
- Encouraging
- Sharing ideas
- Serving as a model
- Raising questions
- Guiding discussion
- Restating ideas and capturing ideas
- Challenging thinking
- Energising

Considering some of the practicalities above we have:

Climate. We've looked at the physical climate in the terms of monitoring the temperature of the room, ventilation etc. There is also an intellectual climate and emotional climate to consider. For example, the charity *Action for Happiness* is adamant that the best path to a happier world is evidence-based and eschews other paths such as that offered by the 'law of attraction', Shamanism or metaphysical approaches. It would probably be worth clarifying your own position on this as it will affect the intellectual climate of the workshop. At least as important, however, is the emotional climate. Generally, people learn best when they feel secure and supported. If participants feel they can make mistakes without being 'punished' (by criticism or mocking etc) then they will be more likely to take the sort of personal risks that lead to significant learning. It also helps if participants feel you actually care about them and their learning. There is an old adage amongst good teachers that "they don't care how much you know, until they know how much you care". If participants are convinced that you care about them and their happiness then they will be much more receptive to what you have to offer.

Listening. One of the most valuable things a facilitator can do is to listen actively to participants. You won't be able to do this well if there is a dialogue going on inside your own head about what you're going to say next. Active listening means not only hearing what the participants have to say but letting them know that they've been heard. You can do this subtly with nods in the right places and you can do it more powerfully by reflecting back the cognitive and emotional content of what the participants say. People who are trained as counsellors and other helping professions learn how to listen actively and for this reason they often make very good workshop facilitators. If you don't have any background in listening actively then you might want to consider doing a workshop on active listening or even a short course on counselling skills in which listening skills play a major role.

Encouraging. By your comments and feedback you can encourage a participant to contribute and say more. As well as positive comments, active use of body language including facial expressions, nodding and eye contact can all serve to encourage participants. Thanking participants for their contributions and their participation encourages other participants to contribute also.

Sharing. How many of the experiences you've had listening to lectures or talks or presentations (with or without Power-Point slides) have been life-changing or riveting or real learning experiences? 'Very few' is the answer most people give to this question. So our advice is to keep the 'lecturing' to a minimum in your happiness workshop. Our rule of thumb is to lecture only if we can't think of another way of conveying the ideas and information we want participants to have. You'll find lots of activities in this book for alternative ways of conveying ideas and information about happiness.

Serving as a model. Even if you are running a happiness workshop no-one will expect you to be exuding joy one hundred per cent of the time. But participants will expect you to practice what you preach – and that includes being cheerful most of the time. In a workshop, facilitators act as a model in other ways too. Participants will look to the facilitator who is leading the workshop to model behaviours and attitudes. This includes, for example, starting on time after breaks. So one of the roles of a facilitator in a happiness workshop is to act as a model participant.

Asking questions. Questions are a powerful source of learning. The answers we get in life depend critically on the questions we ask or get asked. So when people are asked different questions it can lead to significant learning.

In some of the activities it will be necessary to use questions to distil learning from the activity or distil additional learning. For example, there is an activity on contributions to knowledge about happiness ('*Some Facts about Happiness*') in which participants are asked about what they see as the most important facts on that list and this will cause them to think harder about these contributions to knowledge and they will learn which, for them, are most significant.

Many of the activities in this book end with a plenary session and usually the most powerful thing a facilitator can do in a plenary session is to ask the participants questions about their experience of the activity.

Guiding discussion. How far should you let the discussion get off-topic? On the one hand a discussion that seems to be digressing may just be a reflection of what the participants wish to be learning. If it seems to be addressing learning aims that participants disclosed at the start of the workshop then letting it run can make a lot of sense. On the other hand if it seems to be unproductive or reflects one participant riding a particular hobby-horse then it is probably time to bring the discussion back on track. And one of the best ways of guiding a discussion is, again, by asking questions.

Restating ideas and capturing ideas. As a facilitator there are times when it is helpful to reflect back to a participant what they have said by paraphrasing it in your own words. This can be useful for checking for understanding and for clarifying. It also lets the participant know they've been heard and it can be useful for emphasising a really valuable point. Sometimes it's appropriate for a facilitator to summarise the key elements of a conversation up to that point. This can be particularly helpful in ending one phase of the conversation and moving on the next or simply ending a discussion following a particular workshop activity.

Challenging thinking. The most effective way of challenging thinking is probably, yet again, questioning. Socratic dialogue, for example, is all about realising significant learning by means of questioning.

For example, when a participant makes a generalisation the facilitator can ask for specific examples. It's also possible to test an assertion by asking whether it is supported by the experience of the other participants. Questioning the assumption(s) on which a participant's contribution is based is another example.

There are also likely to be times when you may want to simply challenge the accuracy of a participant's statement. There are many myths surrounding happiness and there is much research that challenges these myths. This is the focus, for example, of a whole book by Sonja Lyubomirsky, *The Myths of Happiness*. The more evidence-based knowledge you acquire about happiness the better the position you'll be in to challenge inaccurate statements about happiness.

Energising. Be sensitive to the energy levels of the participants. All you really have to work with in a workshop is the participants' attention and their energy. So it's important to maintain energy levels, and if they start to sag to introduce something which will lift them. Here are some ideas:

- Ask the participants to do something that will take them a little outside their comfort zones. Energy levels are contagious so it may be sufficient for you to energise only some of the participants. For example, a 'round' will do this for many of the participants as it has an element of speaking in public.
- Ask participants to do something that is new to most of them. For example, there is an activity called 'Portraits' in this book which will be new to most of the participants and will therefore serve to raise energy levels.
- Model high energy yourself in your body movements, tone of voice and pace of the workshop.

Getting ready to go – the end part

The main elements of the last stage of a workshop involve capturing the lessons, turning the learning into actions and ending the workshop.

Capturing the lessons. One workshop pitfall is to design and facilitate a happiness workshop that is an enjoyable experience but which has little impact on the actual learning of the participants. To avoid this, it is worth paying particular attention to distilling, consolidating and reinforcing some of the learning.

Turning learning into actions. It's one thing to learn about happiness and another to turn that learning into happier lives. The purpose of your workshop is probably to help participants live happier lives and share that happiness with others. Doing that is likely to depend on the participants actually taking some action after the workshop. This is why we've included an action planning activity in this book.

Ending the workshop. It's much better to end the workshop with a bang than a whimper. You're unlikely to feel happy about your workshop if it ends with participants slipping away individually with only a minority staying until the end. So give some thought to how you can bring the workshop to a successful conclusion and end on a high note. Here are some ideas to avoid a 'fizzle-out' finish:

- End promptly. It's much better to end 5 minutes early than 5 minutes late.
- Don't try to use the last 45 minutes trying to say all the things you planned to say during the workshop.
- Return to the aims of the workshop and the expectations/aims of the participants and remind them what's been covered and what they've done.
- Don't include an 'any other business' session at the end of the workshop. This is tempting as it's the way that meetings often finish but a workshop is not a meeting; it has a different purpose and serves different ends.
- Plan a final session in which all the participants make a contribution. A round of learning points or actions of 'next steps' kind can contribute to a very effective conclusion. 'Rounds' can be very effective and we've suggested (above) a round of learning points or actions of the 'next steps' kind as a conclusion.
- Thank the participants. Express your appreciation for their work in the workshop and their contribution to realising the aims of the workshop. One of the activities in this book ('Aims and

Guidance') refers to 'participation', 'experimentation', 'reflection' and 'contribution'. You could thank the participants for their efforts in all of those dimensions.
- Do something at the end that participants will appreciate as really important. For example, you could give the participants a handout with a summary of the main things you've covered and /or particularly important lessons.
- Do something active at the end. If, for example, you've included a session of action planning towards the end then you could ask participants to compare their planned actions ... or their next steps.

After the workshop

As soon as the workshop ends some participants will have to rush off to another commitment or catch a bus or train. You can help the other participants get more from the workshop by encouraging them to stay around and talk further to each other or to you. You can support this by providing tea/coffee/juice/water at the end for those who want to stay and talk. You can also encourage them to swap contact details and stay in touch as they share an interest in finding and spreading happiness.

No matter how you feel the happiness workshop has gone it can always get better. The main way we get better at things is by finding out what went well and what went less well.

A straightforward way of doing this is simply to think back over the workshop and write down whatever comes to mind under the following headings:
1. The 3 things I liked best about the workshop
2. What I think are the 3 main opportunities for further development of the workshop.

This is best done as soon after the workshop as possible. You should also ask participants to evaluate the workshop as their feedback will be invaluable. We have made some suggestions about doing this in the activity 'Simple Feedback Form'.

Finally, some notes for novices

We end this chapter by addressing the situation faced by someone who is very new to running a happiness workshop. Suppose you have become fascinated by the new evidence-based knowledge about happiness and you want to use workshops to help more people to benefit. However, you've never run a happiness workshop before and you are drawn to do so - this last section is for you.

The core aims of a happiness workshop are likely to centre around: (1) conveying some of that knowledge, preferably in an experiential way, (2) directly enhancing the mood of the participants (i.e. they should feel happier at the end of the workshop) and (3) supporting the commitment on the part of all, or nearly all, of the participants to test out some new behaviours which research has found can enhance sustainable happiness. If you are completely new to running happiness workshops then our main advice is to simply choose the activities that you feel most comfortable and confident using.

Do we have any other advice for someone new to running happiness workshops? Here are five suggestions that you might find useful:

1. Attend other workshops as a participant, preferably happiness workshops if you can find them.

2. When you attend other people's workshops then critically review the experience afterwards. Rather than simply having a think about the experience you can use the format we

suggest above for replanning your own workshop i.e. '3 things I liked best and 3 main opportunities for further development'.

3. Run the workshop with someone else. There are many advantages to doing this, including:

- It means that you will have someone with whom to share workshop tasks, including the preparation and organisation. And that can reduce the stress of putting on a happiness workshop.
- You will have someone working with you with different strengths. Some people are better at organising and managing workshops and others are better at 'pure' facilitation and interacting with a group. With two people you can each play to your strengths.
- You will have someone to act as a sounding board to test out your ideas and perceptions of what is going on and how to handle it.
- The amount of facilitation skill and other resources available to the group is greater with two people. Two heads are better than one, four eyes are better than two and four ears are better than two.
- A second person can act as trouble-shooter for handling difficulties that individual participants might experience to minimise any impact on the rest of the group, such as the departure from the workshop of a participant whose child has become ill.
- You can lead activities in sequence. This would mean that when one person is facilitating an activity the other person could be concentrating on being fully prepared for the next activity.

4. Find a more experienced facilitator to work with. This is an extension of the last idea but in this case you'll be the apprentice and you'll be in a support role rather than leading the workshop.

5. Do some serious study on running workshops. You can find material on the web worth reading – as always, when seeking knowledge on the web, please be discriminating. You can also find books written on the subject of how to run workshops, such as:

- Nikki Sims (2006) *How to run a great workshop: The complete guide to designing and running brilliant workshops and meetings* (Pearson Business)
- Rob Yeung (2002) *Making workshops work: Ensure your workshops create high-octane interaction* (HowToBooks)
- Robert Chalmers (2002) *Participatory workshops: A sourcebook of 21 sets of ideas and activities* (Routledge)
- Kimberley Hare (2005) *The trainer's toolkit: Bringing brain-friendly learning to life* (Crown House Publishing)
- Alan Matthews (2012) *How to design and deliver great training* (Create Space)

Conclusion

In this chapter we've looked at what a happiness workshop is and is not, the stages of such a workshop, running it, designing, managing and facilitating it as well as tips for those who have never run a happiness workshop before. We'd like to end the chapter by emphasising that if you intend to run your workshop again the best way to improve it is to revise it as soon as you reasonably can after the end to take on board lessons from what went well and what you can improve next time.

Activity 1
Extraordinary Achievements

Action for Happiness Key
Emotion, Direction, Relating

An ice-breaker for pairs and groups

Rationale

This is a very effective activity to use as an icebreaker for a number of reasons. Firstly, it captures the participants' attention and strengthens their self-belief and motivation. Secondly, it lets the participants know what resources there are in the room amongst the other participants. And finally it enables the participants to feel good about themselves and what they bring to the workshop.

The main aim of this ice-breaker activity is to engage the attention of the participants.

Materials

None required.

Process/procedure

1. Explain that the room you are in represents the months of the year arranged in a rough circle, starting with January 1 on one side of the door and proceeding through the seasons – winter, spring, summer, autumn – round the four walls until you reach December and New Year's Eve on the other side of the door.

2. Tell the group to stand in their 'birthday position'. With groups of about 2 dozen or more you may have 'birthday twins': two people who share a birthday – though probably not the same year of birth.

3. Arrange the participants in 'birthday pairs' with the nearest, starting from January.

4. Ask them to talk to each other about two things: (1) something extraordinary they have already achieved in their lives, and (2) something extraordinary they dream of doing, having or being in the future.

Plenary/debrief

Ask for feedback from people who have been touched, moved or inspired by their partners (and usually they all are). Then ask them to sit down again - in their birthday pairs.

Notes including comments and variations

What this exercise does is to secure attention, and start the priming process of developing self-belief and strengthening motivation.

Activity 2
Happiness Journal

Action for Happiness Key
Emotion, Direction, Appreciating

Individual, group, brainstorming

Rationale
This exercise is intended to introduce participants to the practice of keeping a happiness journal as a tool that they can use throughout the workshop and beyond to capture insights, ideas, lessons, reflections and knowledge about happiness that they feel are likely to be most useful to them now and in the future.

Materials
A smart notebook given to all participants (as a surprise gift).

Process/procedure
1. Explain the rationale for this process (as above).

2. Hand out the notebooks as presents to the participants. This itself is a mood-enhancer as people generally like to receive gifts.

3. Ask participants to initiate their new happiness notebook by (1) writing their name in it, (2) making a note of at least one happy experience, (3) drafting an email to someone they would like to thank for making a positive contribution to their life, big or small. Mention that participants can also use it as a diary to record what makes them happy, perhaps for the next 2 weeks to see the effect (people who keep such a diary are often surprised at the results). They can also use it to record their self-reflections or observations to any of the activities they do as part of this happiness workshop.

4. Emphasise that the notebook is a working document to capture the ideas, insights, thoughts, feelings, lessons, conclusions, pieces of knowledge etc that relate to their happiness. This will help them study their own happiness.

5. Have a mini-brainstorm to find 21 things people might write in their happiness journal.

6. Facilitators should also refer to the happiness journal during the rest of the workshop – so that participants don't forget about them or forget to use them

Plenary/debrief
- How could you best use your happiness journal to get most value from it?

Activity 3
42 Varieties of Happiness

Action for Happiness Key
***Trying out,
Appreciating,
Direction***

Group, brainstorming

Rationale

The main purpose of this activity is to explore the many different ways there are to be happy. At the same time it will develop a resource for the rest of the workshop (e.g. the Biography activity), and help participants think about happiness in all its many forms.

Materials

Flip chart, flip chart stand and flip chart pens

Process/procedure

1. Introduce the activity: our task is to find 42 varieties of happiness and we'll use brainstorming to achieve this. And indicate the reasons for doing this (see above).

2. Introduce the concept of brainstorming i.e. to generate a wide range of ideas and make sure participants understand the basic 'rules' of brainstorming (see appendix 1 for further details). Repeat that the goal of this activity is to find 42 varieties of happiness by using brainstorming.
Here is a starter for 5:
- Bliss
- Cheerfulness
- Contentment
- Delight
- Ecstasy

So now our task is to brainstorm 32 more varieties of happiness. And we'll be using the results later in the workshop. Brainstorm answers to the question: 'What different forms can happiness take?'

Plenary/debrief

Very brief discussion based on questions along the lines of:
- Which 2 kinds of happiness do you find easiest to access and why?
- Which 2 kinds do you find most difficult to access and why?
- Which varieties of happiness do most want to access more and why?
- Ask participants to make some notes in their happiness journals.

Notes including comments and variations

When recording the contributions to the brainstorm, use a range of different, brightly coloured, pens. Pin the result of the brainstorm around the walls for later.

Activity 4
Support Network

Action for Happiness Key
Relating, Direction

Individual, pairs

Rationale

There is growing scientific evidence that people with good support networks are happier than people without them. The purpose of this activity is to help participants explore how well developed their own support network is and to give them an opportunity to consider what actions they could take to develop it further.

Materials

Enough copies of the handout for all the participants

Process/procedure

1. Provide participants with copies of the handout.

2. Allow enough time (about 10 minutes) for the participants to complete the sections individually.

3. Ask participants to discuss their results in pairs (preferably made up of people who don't know each other). They can discuss the detail of what they have written or the generalisations they draw from it. (5 mins)

Plenary/debrief

What do you notice about your collection of names? For example:
- Are you relying on the same person or persons for many different types of advice or help?
- Are you better connected where you work or outside of work?
- Are there any other kinds of support you get from other people?
- What types of support do you find it easy to ask for? Why is that?
- Are there any types of support that you find it difficult to ask for? If so, why is that, and how might you make it easier?
- Are there any gaps, and if so, how might you fill them?
- Are there any actions to take as a result of what you found out in this activity? If so, make a note of them on your handout or in your happiness journal.

Handout: Personal Networks

Write down the names of the people you consult and talk to on each of the following questions. Who can I...

	Inside my work or community group	Outside my work or community group
...go to for general sharing and catching up?		
...ask about specialist information in my particular field?		
...ask about solutions to issues and problems?		
... get help from with thinking through a particularly difficult issue or question?		
... get approval and validation for a course of action I am thinking of taking?		
...ask for advice about a tricky moral or political issue?		
...tell good news to?		
...tell bad news to?		
...share a secret with?		
... take a risk with?		
... just say 'hello' to and keep in touch from time to time?		

Activity 5
Biography

Action for Happiness Key
Resilience, Acceptance, Meaning

Individual, pairs

Rationale

The aim of this exercise is to reflect on life experiences to date, and to learn what enhances happiness. At the same time, participants will get an opportunity to savour past experiences of happiness and discover what they can do to enhance happiness now and in the future.

Materials

A large sheet of flip chart paper and a copy of the 'biography' handout. A range of coloured pens for participants to use in drawing their lifelines.

Process/procedure

1. Provide each participant with a copy of the handout.

2. Take a sheet of flip chart paper and create a graph with 'time' on the bottom axis and 'feelings' up the side.

3. Read the handout and raise any questions about it. Then follow the guidelines on the handout.

4. Try to create a sentence or two that summarises your distinctive pattern of experience.

5. Find another participant, preferably someone you don't know, and talk about your lifelines.

Plenary/debrief

Base the plenary on questions such as:
- What did you discover when you drew your lifeline?
- What were your most enjoyable, positive, meaningful or happy experiences?
- Could you see any pattern?
- Were there any surprises?
- Was there significant learning in this for you?

Notes including comments and variations

Individuals may want to simply look at each other's lifelines rather than talk about or explain them. Note that it is possible to start the lifeline at some point later than birth (e.g. at the point of leaving school) to avoid going too deeply into their past.

Handout: Biography

1. Look back over your life so far and note down events that come to mind. Start where you are now and work backwards.

2. Sort the events you noted into chronological order

3. Draw a graph on a large sheet of paper (A4 or A3) with time on the bottom axis and feelings up the side as follows:

4. Plot the events of your life in chronological order. When you were feeling good you have a peak, when you were feeling low there will be a trough.

5. Look back over your lifeline starting from the beginning and coming forward to the present. Can you find periods and give them a label that describes how they were, what they felt like and their purpose? Mark these periods on your lifeline.

6. Can you see any themes emerging? A theme might be:
    - a pattern of thoughts, feelings or behaviour or actions
    - an aspect of your life that seems to be there all the time.
    - an aspect of your life that makes itself apparent from time to time.
   Identify and list such themes.

7. Focusing on the peaks:
    - What did 2 or more of the peaks have in common?
    - What did 2 or more of the peaks have that made them different?
    - Take one or two of the troughs and look at the journey from the trough to the next peak.
   What did you do to create, assist or allow that movement?

8. If your lifeline was somebody else's and s/he was describing it to you, how would you react to it?
    - What would you think about it?
    - What would you feel?
    - What do you see as that person's unfinished business or next goals?
    - What decisions need to be taken?

Activity 6
Strengths Brainstorm

Action for Happiness Key
Emotion, Acceptance

Individual, group, brainstorming

Rationale

There is growing psychological evidence that identifying and playing to our strengths contributes more to our happiness and well-being than focussing on overcoming our weaknesses or deficits. The aim of this activity is to help participants discover more of their strengths and to feel good in the process.

Materials

Flip chart, flip chart stand and flip chart pens plus pen and paper or happiness journal or smart phone for note-taking

Process/procedure

1. Introduce the activity: our task is to create a list of positive characteristics of people, grounded in our experience of them. Then indicate the reasons for doing this activity (as above).

2. Think of someone you like and admire, and what you like and admire about them.

3. Introduce the concept of brainstorming i.e. to generate a wide range of ideas and introduce the basic 'rules' of brainstorming (see appendix).

4. What are the positive qualities of people we like and admire? – brainstorm the answers.

5. Now identify 4 positive qualities from the list we've generated that apply to a greater or lesser extent to you, and note them down.

6. Add 2 more positive qualities that apply to you that are not on our list.

7. End with a round where each person shares one positive quality that applies to them (preferably one that is not shared by others in the room i.e. one that is yours alone and makes you special).

8. Ask participants to make a note of their strengths and other positive attributes in their happiness journals.

Plenary/debrief

None required.

Activity 7
Appreciation

Action for Happiness Key
Appreciating

Individual, small groups

Rationale

Scientific studies have found that expressing gratitude for the good things in your life has a positive impact on well-being. Recent research by Seligman and his colleagues suggest that expressing gratitude not only increases happiness but also reduces depressive symptoms over the medium term. Human beings are predisposed to notice the negative things in life (which psychologists call the 'negativity bias). This activity will help the participants recognise things they appreciate in each of the key areas in life and help to overcome the innate negativity bias by focussing their thinking on the positive elements in their lives. Anyone with coaching experience will recognise the similarities to the 'Wheel of Life' activity.

Materials

Handout: Appreciation.

Process/procedure

1. Introduce the activity by explaining the importance of expressing gratitude for the good things in one's life, and the nature of the negativity bias. Explain that this activity will give participants the opportunity to examine different aspects of their lives and to decide which elements they appreciate most.

2. For most people each of the following are important dimensions in life:
   - Physical health
   - Family
   - Social
   - Recreation/leisure
   - Work/job/profession/career
   - Material resources
   - Self-development/education
   - Inner self

3. Ask participants to make a note on the handout of two things they appreciate or feel grateful for in each of the dimensions, and why.

4. Ask them to find two other people and share what they've written in each of the dimensions and note anything that their partners have come up with in a category that they are also grateful for.

Plenary/debrief

Discussion based on what others have come up with that also applies to you.
How difficult was it to come up with things that you are grateful for in your life? Why was that?

Notes including comments and variations

Instead of doing stage 2 in groups go straight to the plenary. Ask people for some of the things they've come up with in each of the areas. Write up on a flip chart. Collect about five items in each category.

Handout: Appreciation

Physical health	Family	Social	Recreation/Leisure

Work/job/profession/career	Material resources	Self-development/education	Inner self

Activity 8
Have a Good Day

Action for Happiness Key
Emotion, Direction

Individual, pairs

Rationale

According to psychologist and expert on savouring Fred Bryant, our happiness doesn't depend only on our capacity to feel pleasure, but also on our capacity to find it, regulate it, manipulate it and sustain it. This is why being able to savour (i.e. thoughts or behaviours which generate, intensify or prolong feelings of enjoyment) is so important. Savouring comes in many forms, and can be focussed on the past (e.g. reminiscence), the present or the future (e.g. anticipation).

This activity is all about creating a vision of a happy time in the future which can provide direction and motivation, in other words, it gives workshop participants the opportunity to use their imagination and practice anticipating (savouring) a happy future.

Materials

Flip chart, pen and paper or happiness journal or smart phone for taking notes.

Process/procedure

1. Ask participants to think about what for them would constitute an ideal day in the future, say, a year in the future. What would make such a day memorable or good or even wonderful? Think about the morning, the afternoon and the evening. What exactly would you be doing? With whom? And then jot down some notes if you want to.

2. Find a partner and each take 5 minutes in turn telling your partner about what for you would be an ideal day in the future.

Plenary/debrief

- What would make your day especially good?
- Collect elements of different people's ideal days on a flip chart ... and then note similarities and differences.
- Can we improve our ideal day in the future by using elements of other people's ideal day in the future?
- How can we use our knowledge about sources of happiness (see the introductory chapters for more information) to improve our ideal day in the future?
- What can you do to make it more likely you'll realise your ideal day in the future?
- How can you get more the elements of your ideal day into the rest of your days in the future?

Activity 9
Group Shoulder Massage

Action for Happiness Key
Giving, Appreciating, Emotion, Relating

Group

Rationale

There is plenty of scientific evidence that doing things for other people isn't just good for their well-being, it makes us feel good too. The New Economics Foundation (NEF - see references and resources for the website details) lists 'giving' as one of the 'Five Ways to Well-Being'. Giving need not be a chore! Doing something nice for a friend or a stranger is a great way to give. This simple physical activity allows participants to practice giving, as well as to practice receiving and expressing gratitude.

The main aim of this activity is to give participants an opportunity to give and receive and reflect on its impact on their happiness.

Materials

None required.

Process/procedure

1. Ask the group to form a circle with each person standing next to someone of similar height. Then ask each person to place their hands on the shoulders of the person in front of them. Each person then gives the person in front of them a shoulder massage. Encourage feedback to the massage giver (e.g. "that's really nice").

2. After a couple of minutes ask the group to do an about-face so they are now massaging the shoulders of the person who just gave them a massage.

3. Ask participants to express their appreciation to those on either side of them in an appropriate way.

Plenary/debrief

This can lead to a discussion on relaxation, touch, giving and receiving and/or trust. It can also be an end-of-group activity. You can lead the plenary with questions like:

- How did it feel to receive a shoulder massage?
- How did it feel to give a shoulder massage?
- How did it feel to express your appreciation?
- How did it feel to be appreciated?
- How can you get more appreciation in your life?
- How can you get more giving and receiving in your life?
- What did you learn from this experience?

Activity 10
Giving Compliments

Action for Happiness Key
Giving, Appreciating, Emotion, Relating

Small groups

Rationale

Giving genuine compliments is a remarkably effective way to create a positive atmosphere between people, to develop good relationships and to make people feel good about themselves. One of the reasons why sincere compliments, delivered well, are so powerful is that they tell the person being complimented that we notice them and that we value them. Recent research also suggests that giving specific praise about task performance can help improve it.

But compliments are not just good for the receiver, they are also good for the giver because they require us to turn our attention to the positive, and every time we do that we're rising above our inbuilt negativity bias. The more we give compliments or praise, the easier it gets to notice positive attributes about other people, whether that's their appearance, their behaviour or their strengths, and the less attention we give the negative things about life.

Materials

Flip chart or handout of some examples, or a copy of the VIA questionnaire for each participant from pages 243-265 of Martin Seligman's book 'Flourish' or downloaded from: www.authentichappiness.org or from www.viastrengths.org.
Post-It notes are required for variations.

Process/procedure

1. Just before lunch-time number people off to produce groups of three (so, for example, if there are 24 participants then count round the room to eight then start again). This should ensure that most of the participants are with people that they don't know very well.

2. Invite each group of three to go for a walk before lunch and while they do so to give each of their partners two pieces of positive feedback about what they have brought to this workshop ... and to give examples if possible:

Examples:
- Sense of humour
- Said something that inspired or enthused
- 'Give it a go' attitude
- Good listener
- Showed bravery/curiosity
- Shared their experience
- Took the lead in the group
- Did some kind or generous act
- Cheerfulness

It might be helpful to put these examples on a flip chart or a handout.

Plenary/debrief

Ask participants to share how they felt getting compliments from relative strangers.

Ask participants how the giving and receiving of these small tokens of appreciation made a difference to their relationship.

Ask participants to consider how they might give more compliments to family, friends, colleagues, strangers in future and have them make notes in their happiness journals.

Notes including comments and variations

One great way to vary this activity is to ask participants to write compliments with examples anonymously on Post-It notes, as many compliments as they can think of for as many participants as possible. Ask them to stick each Post-It to the back of the relevant person. When everyone has finished, every participant should have some compliments on Post-Its which they can savour, and keep in their happiness journals as reminders of the day.

You could also focus solely VIA Strengths, and have participants notice and write down on Post-It notes the VIA Strengths that they have seen others exhibit, with examples. For this, it might be helpful to have the VIA Strengths written up on flip charts or on a handout.

Activity 11
Past & Future Achievements

Action for Happiness Key
Emotion, Direction, Appreciating

Individual

Rationale

It's very easy to forget about your past achievements and how good they made you feel, particularly if you're very focussed on the future, wrapped up in goals and targets and busy ticking things off your 'To Do' list. This activity provides an opportunity to savour achievements and successes from the past, as well as those to look forward to, and to find out what you can learn from them. It also provides a resource that will be valuable when you encounter difficult times in the future.

The main aim of this activity is to focus the attention of participants on their achievements, to savour them and to enjoy anticipating their future achievements.

Materials

Happiness journal or paper and pen/pencil

Process/procedure

Divide your life to date into 3 equal parts

E.g. if you were 57 then it would look like this:

1---------------------------19-------------------------38-------------------------57

2. (5 mins) For each of the three parts list 3 achievements.

3. (5 mins) Think of 3 achievements you want in the next 10 years.

4. (15 mins) Share the results with 2 other people (preferably people you don't know).
As you do so, see if you have any particular achievements in common or any successes listed by your partners that could also apply to you.

Plenary/debrief

Some questions from the following:

- What do you notice about your achievements/successes?
- How do you feel when you look at your past achievements/successes?
- What lessons can you draw from your past achievements/successes that will help you achieve §what you want to in the next 10 years?

Activity 12
Basic Relaxation

Action for Happiness Key
Emotion

Individual

Rationale

When we talk about happiness, our thoughts often go immediately to the high arousal positive emotions such as elation, joy or excitement. But there is a whole category of low arousal positive emotions related to relaxation, such as calm, serenity and tranquillity, which are just as important for well-being. This activity is a straightforward exercise to practice relaxation, which will help participants feel good and provide them with a tool they can use in various contexts in their lives. Although breathing exercises are generally very simple, they're not necessarily easy to do, so practice is a good thing. Relaxation also aids visualisation so this exercise would be a good precursor to any visualisation activity, any involving imagination or having happy thoughts about the past or the future.

Materials

None required.

Process/procedure

Lead participants through the following steps:

1. With your eyes closed, give your attention to your breathing, counting the duration of each in-breath and each out-breath.

2. After doing that for several breaths then lengthen your in-breath and your out-breath a little, allowing your breathing to deepen as you do so. Then repeat, increasing the duration of in-breath and out-breath a little more, again breathing a little more deeply. Continue increasing the length so long as it feels comfortable to do so, then maintain these longer breaths for 4 minutes.

3. Slightly increase the length of the out-breath and give most attention to the longer out-breath in this exercise. Continue for four more minutes then open your eyes.

Plenary/debrief

- What happened to you in that experience?
- What thoughts came into your head?
- How did you feel while you were doing it?
- How do you feel now?
- When can you use this relaxation tool in your life?

Notes including comments and variations

Proceed directly from this activity to one using visualisation or imagination.

Activity 13
Purpose

Action for Happiness Key
Direction, Acceptance, Meaning

Individual, pairs

Rationale

Although discussions about meaning and purpose in life have taken place since the dawn of time, it's only relatively recently that scientific research has been carried out on these topics and their connection with happiness. Being clear about purpose and direction in life contributes significantly to happiness and life satisfaction. The objective for doing this exercise is to help you clarify your larger purpose and direction.

Materials

Several sheets of A4 paper per participant, happiness journal for reflections.

Process/procedure

1. (2 mins) Draw the largest circle you can on a sheet of A4 paper. Then draw another one within it, about half the diameter.
2. (5 mins) In the outer circle list the character strengths that you feel you have.
3. (2 mins) In the inner circle list three other positive aspects of yourself.
4. (10 mins) Do the following steps on a separate sheet of paper:
    a. Take two of your positive qualities that you value most highly.
    b. List one or two ways in which you enjoy expressing those positive qualities.
    c. Imagine that the world out there were perfect. What would it be like? Describe it in the present tense in a sentence (or two).
    d. Put together your answer to each of the above three parts. A good formula for combining your answers is: I am ... as I ... in order to...

Play around with the words until you get something which feels congruent. Don't worry if it doesn't feel right straight away – just play around with it. Warning: your sentence may sound really slushy!

Example:
    a. The two qualities I value most highly: Being open-minded and innovative.
    b. Two ways I enjoy expressing these positive qualities: discovering new things and then sharing them.
    c. A perfect world: Everyone is joyful and at peace with themselves.
    d. I am open-minded and innovative as I discover and share new ways of helping people (including me) find more joy and peace in their (our) lives.

5. (10 mins) Share the result with another participant. Their role is to help you reflect on any way(s) in which you could use your life to contribute in any way to that purpose.

6. (5 mins) Spend 5 minutes noting down your reflections in your happiness journal.

Plenary/debrief

Ask participants to share their purpose statements and/or their reflections with the group.

Activity 14
Loving Kindness Meditation

Action for Happiness Key
Emotion, Acceptance, Relating

Individual

Rationale

Scientific research has shown that loving-kindness meditation makes a significant contribution to happiness. It can actually change the brain (e.g. see Davidson & Begley, 2013). Buddhist monk Matthieu Ricard, who has been called 'the happiest person in the world', ascribes his happiness to his practice of loving-kindness meditation. The purpose of this activity is to practice this form of meditation.

Materials

A flipchart or white board might be useful to write up the mantra.

Process/procedure

1. Sit comfortably with your eyes closed and just notice your breathing.

2. Think of someone you care a lot about. Then use your internal voice to repeat the following words:
   - May you be safe
   - May you be healthy
   - May you be happy
   - May you be peaceful

3. Think of someone else you care about and slowly repeat the mantra as you think of them. Keep doing this with other people in your life for about 2 minutes.

4. Then direct the phrases towards yourself with the mantra:
   - May I be safe
   - May I be healthy
   - May I be happy
   - May I be peaceful

   Continue for 1 minute.

5. Then direct the phrases towards someone you feel neutral about, possibly someone in this room (or if you already care about everyone in the room then someone at work, a neighbour, someone you see occasionally at the shops, a distant relative etc). Continue for 1 minute.

6. Think of someone you don't like e.g. someone who has given you a hard time. Direct your thoughts of loving kindness towards that person – for 1 minute.

7. Finally direct the phrases to everybody universally for 2 minutes: May we all be safe etc.

Plenary/debrief

None required.

Activity 15
Sharing Good News

Action for Happiness Key
Relating, Emotion

Pairs

Rationale

Sharing our good news with other people who respond with genuine interest and enthusiasm can increase our positive emotions and help build a stronger relationship between us. Psychologists refer to this as 'capitalising'. By helping other people capitalise on their good news by expressing interest and enthusiasm in what they're saying, you will also help them achieve greater happiness and improve your relationship.

Materials

None required.

Process/procedure

1. Form pairs. Partner A spends 3 minutes sharing some good news with partner B. Partner B concentrates on responding with real and positive interest to whatever good news is shared, i.e. responding by listening actively, respecting, reacting favourably, asking questions.

2. Change roles and this time partner B spends 3 minutes sharing good news with partner A, who concentrates on listening actively, asking questions and responding with positive interest and enthusiasm.

Plenary/debrief

- What sorts of good news did people share?
- What were you thinking when you did this activity?
- How did it feel to express a positive response to your partner's good news?
- How did it feel to share your good news and get a positive and interested response?

Notes including comments and variations

During each of the 3 minutes the listener can gradually withdraw attention to the point of showing complete disinterest and then gradually return attention and favourable response. By doing this the activity can also teach participants about the value of active listening.

Activity 16
What Do You Notice?

Action for Happiness Key
Appreciating

Individual

Rationale

'Mindfulness' means paying attention to the present, to our thoughts, feelings and actions and to what is going on around us, without judgement. This activity allows us to explore different ways of practicing mindfulness, to discover new ways of looking at the world around us, and to develop a creative and playful approach to life.

Materials

Happiness journal or paper and pen (optional)
Camera (optional)
Small bag to put things in (optional)
A map (optional)
Watches (optional)

Process/procedure:

1. Introduce this activity as an experiment in being more engaged with the here and now. It can take place in a green or urban space.
Initiate a brief discussion about what mindfulness is.
The activity can be carried out in a group or individually. As participants to choose what they would like from the following two sections, and agree on a time and a final meeting place (and route if necessary). Reiterate the reasons for doing this activity: to focus our attention on the world around us.

2. Choose your focus before you begin your adventure, for example:
   - All things I notice
   - Small found objects to collect that grab your attention
   - Round/square/bendy/metal/spherical etc., things
   - Blue/red/purple/green/silver/gold/yellow etc., things
   - Smells
   - Sounds
   - Light and shadow
   - Overheard conversations
   - Natural things
   - Man-made things
   - People's shoes
   - Anything else that takes your fancy as a focus...

3. Choose how you would like to document your findings:
   - Simply in your own mind, in the moment
   - By writing things down in any way you wish
   - By drawing them

- By photographing them
- By collecting them – if this is suitable and things are free/paid for.
- In any other documentation style you can think of…

4. Plan your route and set the amount of time you would like to do this activity for:
- Use your map or simply wander and follow your nose
- Set an alarm or let time disappear
- Or anywhere in between…

5. Take your focus + your documentation tools + your plan of action and take yourself out for a mindful adventure and see what you find.

Plenary/debrief:

When the group comes back together at the allotted time, initiate a discussion about how they found it:
- What did you notice?
- How did it feel noticing this?
- Would you like to share your documentation?

Activity 17
Playful Haiku Writing

Action for Happiness Key
Appreciating, Emotion

Individual

Rationale

This is a light-hearted activity which encourages creativity, brings humour into everyday life and builds the participants' confidence when they share their haikus. Additionally it will help participants recognise that they can be creative in this way anywhere, using anything as a stimulus.

This activity can also be done in between workshops, with participants sharing their creative output when they return.

Materials

Pen and paper or happiness journal or smart phone for notes.

Process/procedure

A haiku is a Japanese form of poetry. Traditional haikus have one rule: the haiku has only three lines, the first line has five syllables, the second has seven and the third line has five. They don't need to rhyme.

The haiku is about the journey you're on. Some inspiration you might consider: the weather, the light, the people you pass, the feel of your feet on the pavement/pedals, the things you heard, what you're wearing on the journey, the route you're taking, the things you pass.

Be playful! Haikus can be a serious and beautiful form of poetry, but this exercise is about playing, and bringing humour to your haikus, and to your everyday life.

Examples: (created whilst on a cycle commute)

My cycle to work:
Drives me completely berserk
In a good way, yes.

Hercules my dear,
On you I never have fear.
You steel beauty, you.

Plenary/debrief

Encourage participants to share their haikus, either reading them out loud or writing them up, one per flip chart, which you can stick around the room to bring humour to the entire workshop.

Activity 18
Do a Secret Good Deed

Action for Happiness Key
Giving, Relating, Meaning, Emotion

Individual

Rationale

Scientific research has found that, for most people, doing good also makes us feel good. This activity enables us to carry out our own experiment, testing whether this conclusion also applies to helping others secretly.

Materials

Slips of paper, one per participant.

Process/procedure

1. Ask each of the participants to do a secret good deed over the lunch-break. This must be done without attracting any attention to yourself or taking any credit. This doesn't have to be a big deal – for example, it could involve simply picking up some litter in the street or putting a coin in an expired parking meter – but if you feel moved to donate £50 to Oxfam over the phone, don't let us stop you – but it must be done anonymously and secretly. If it's done for a stranger and the stranger sees the good deed the participant should slip away as quietly and as quickly as possible. If done for a family member the recipient shouldn't know who did it. If asked about the deed the participant should feign ignorance or quietly change the subject.

2. When you return from lunch write your good deed on a slip of paper (provided).

3. The facilitator collects all the slips of paper and reads out the good deeds randomly.

Plenary/debrief

- How did it feel to hear about the good deeds?
- How did if feel doing the good deed?
- How does it feel now to have contributed to this list of good deeds?

Activity 19
Gratitude, Appreciation and Thankfulness

Action for Happiness Key
Appreciating, Giving, Relating, Meaning

Individual

Rationale
Scientific research suggests that expressing gratitude, for example, thanking a person who has done something for you, is an effective way of increasing your own happiness. This activity invites participants to express their appreciation to others, and in doing so, helps them to develop an 'attitude of gratitude'.

Materials
Pen and paper or happiness journal or smart phone for taking notes.

Process/procedure
1. Ask participants to think of someone who personally did them a significant favour or who has done an act of considerable kindness for their family or their group or for people generally. It could be written to a departed family member or friend

2. Then ask if they really expressed their appreciation, gratitude or thankfulness at the time. And ask them to consider the positive impact of the kindness. Ask them how they themselves feel when they receive an expression of appreciation from someone else?

3. Ask participants to use their journal (or some paper) to write a personal letter of gratitude and appreciation to the individual of their choice.

4. It's best if the letter is personal, detailed and spontaneous rather than formal, general and studied.

5. After drafting the letter give participants a new pristine sheet of paper and an envelope and ask them to write it up neatly in their own handwriting and put it in the envelope and address it as though they were going to send it.

6. Participants can decide whether or not to post their letters of appreciation. In research, people hand-delivered their letters and read them to the person being thanked, but this may not be something your participants want to do.

Plenary/debrief
- How did it feel writing the letter? How do you feel now?
- What did you learn from that experience?
- Who else could you write a gratitude letter to?
- Are you going to send it? ...or deliver it? If not, what will you do with your letter?

Activity 20
Portraits

Action for Happiness Key
Emotion, Relating

Pairs

Rationale

This is a quick and easy activity to do which can raise a lot of laughs. By causing people to make eye contact it can also be helpful to those people who generally aren't comfortable with doing this, at the same time enabling them to feel a little closer to someone else.

Materials

Pen or pencil and a piece of A4 paper per participant

Process/procedure

1. Find a partner

2. Partner A spends 3 minutes drawing partner B's face without looking at the picture they are drawing – this is called 'blind drawing'.

3. Afterwards, partner B reciprocates.

4. Ask participants to label their drawings 'A Portrait of [Name]' at the top and sign it at the bottom and then give it to their partner.

5. Ask participants to discuss this experience with their partner – perhaps what happened, how they felt about what was happening and what they were thinking.

Plenary/debrief

- What did it feel like to look at someone else's face for 3 minutes?
- What did it feel like to be looked at by someone else for 3 minutes?
- It is sometimes said that 'the eyes are the windows of the soul'. What positive qualities did you see when you looked into your partner's eyes?

Notes including comments and variations

You can also do this activity as a simple energiser, to lighten the mood of the workshop. If doing it as an energiser, have participants blind draw simultaneously for one minute and ignore the questions and plenary session.

Activity 21
Inspiration

Action for Happiness Key
Relating, Appreciating

Individual, pairs

Rationale
This activity focuses on finding a role model who can act as a guide to living a happier life, to explore the positive qualities of our role models in seeking a life well lived, and to feel inspired and uplifted by them.

Materials
None required.

Process/procedure
1. Who comes to mind when I ask 'Who do you know with many positive qualities? Who inspires you? Who comes to mind when you hear the words "a life well-lived"? From whom can you draw inspiration, optimism and energy? Is it someone you've known personally? A family member? A relative? A friend? Someone you've worked with ... or for? Alive or dead? It might be someone very successful or someone who seems quite ordinary. ' You could also say that it's fine for participants to choose role models that they've read about in the media, a public figure, a historical character, or a fictional character.

> *"I've always thought of my uncle as someone who exemplifies "a life well-lived". He has always worked hard, yes, and has had many different jobs. He's never been afraid of giving something a go. What I admire about him is that he is invariably upbeat, and doesn't allow the trials of life to get him down. He goes out of his way to help other people and is very generous with his money and his time. He's a natural with children, and they love him too. He's always got time for his own kids and grandkids, well time for everyone. He's a devoted carer for his wife who has a terminal illness, and he even remains upbeat about that. I think he lives every day as if it were their last together. He's down to earth, but at the same time he manages to see the best in everyone. I feel very fortunate to know him. I often find myself thinking "What would Uncle Ted say or do in this situation?'*

2. Find a partner, share your role models and compare the reasons that they inspired you. What are their positive qualities that you respond to?

Plenary/debrief
- Who did you choose as a person who inspires you? Collect the names of about 5-10 people. What were some of the qualities? Collect about 10 of their positive qualities.

- How can you use your inspirational figures as role models to improve your life? (e.g. think about them? Name them in your happiness journal? Find photos of them? Savour memories of them? Read about them, if they are famous? Treat them as your guru. Have imaginary conversations with them? Question them – as in, "What would you do, Mum?")

Activity 22
Tributes

Action for Happiness Key
Meaning, Direction

Individual

Rationale

The purpose of this activity is to surface and clarify what it means to live 'a life well-lived'. Part of the discussion will focus on how living a life of meaning and purpose contributes to our happiness. The activity can also help participants find direction and purpose, and enable them to clarify their values.

Materials

Happiness journals for notes.

Process/procedure

1. Try writing your own tribute. How would you like to be remembered? What would you like to be your legacy? What would you like said about you at a celebration of your life? Think about your life overall, including the parts yet to come. Or, if that is difficult, then think about your 70th Birthday Party. What would you like to be said about you? Here is an example:

> *Pauline was a devoted wife and a loving mother of 3 and grandmother of 4. She was loyal, kind and helpful to many, to strangers as well as to friends, neighbours and the wider community. She gave her time willingly to help others in need, and had an uncanny knack of making friends with everyone. People liked having her around; she was down-to-earth spoke her mind, but she did it in a way which everyone valued, even those she was chastising.*
>
> *Despite a privileged upbringing, she was a 'woman of the people': she had a natural gift for making a connection with others whatever their background. She worked tirelessly in support of young offenders and those in prison, and changed the lives of many. She believed that everyone deserves another chance to turn their lives around, and that education would enable this. She was instrumental in helping many young offenders and prisoners gain good qualifications which helped them find work on their release.*
>
> *In her retirement, she continued helping the most needy on a voluntary basis, organising winter soup kitchens and Christmas shows for the homeless. Pauline really was a 'rare old bird', working energetically for others right up to the end. Her forgiveness, warmth and empathy have made a lasting difference to everyone who knew her.*

2. Write your own tribute in your happiness journal. You may find it easier if you mind-map it first.

Plenary/debrief

- What does your tribute say about what really matters to you?

Activity 23
Rediscovering Happiness

Action for Happiness Key
Giving, Appreciating, Emotion, Relating

Individual, pairs

Rationale
The aim of this activity is to introduce workshop participants to the 10 'Happiness Keys' according to Action for Happiness, and to help participants rediscover things that have brought them happiness in the past.

Materials
None required.

Process/procedure
1. According to the charity Action for Happiness there are 10 keys to finding happiness:
   - Giving i.e. doing things for others
   - Relating, i.e. connecting with people
   - Exercising, i.e. taking care of your body
   - Appreciating, i.e. noticing and valuing the world around
   - Trying out, i.e. continuing to learn new things
   - Direction, i.e. having goals to look forward to
   - Resilience, i.e. finding ways to bounce back
   - Emotion, i.e. taking a positive approach
   - Acceptance, i.e. being comfortable with who you are
   - Meaning, i.e. being part of something bigger.

2. Think of an example in your own life when each of these keys has contributed to your happiness in the past. Here's an example of the first five to give you an idea:

Give: Volunteering at my son's primary school. I was the Treasurer on the PTA for four years, and used to help out at PTA fund-raising events like fetes, cake sales and quiz nights. We raised over £25k, which all went back into the school to pay for extra-curricular treats for the children like trips to the theatre, dance days and an entertainer at the Christmas party. It was very satisfying to feel that you had made a contribution to the education and well-being of the children.

Connect: I belong to a local choral society. It's great to go along to the weekly rehearsals and to have a chin wag with the other singers. I've made some really good friends who I socialise with outside of choir too. It's really enriched my social circle. I can remember thinking about whether I'd like it before I joined, but I'm so glad I did.

Be active: I go running and cycling a couple to times a week. Often my daughter (who lives a few miles away) joins me for the cycle rides. It's a great way to keep fit and keep in touch with my daughter, we chat as we pedal away and I always feel miles better afterwards.

Be curious: I have to travel a fair bit with work. I like food and cooking so I try to sample different cuisines when I'm travelling, going to different restaurants or simply sampling unusual foods on the hotel menu. Last week I had some fabulous Norwegian food. I'm going to have a go at cooking it myself at the weekend. My friends love coming to my house for dinner because they know they'll be trying something new!

Learn: I've just taken up sailing, because my son was keen on it, and I thought I should give it a go. I've never been a great sailor but I'm finding being in control of a little boat is a different experience to being a passenger. Yes I've already capsized! But every time I have a lesson I feel more confident. And I've made a new circle of friends too, which is an added bonus.

3. Choose one of the keys that has contributed to your happiness in the past. Then use it as inspiration for discovering a way to enhance your happiness in the future.

4. Find a partner and compare notes (10 minutes each way).

Plenary/debrief

Which of the 10 keys did you find it most difficult to come up with an example of?

So for the two most difficult key categories let's have a few examples of what some people came up with. Write these up on a flip chart.

Remembering activities that you enjoyed in the past can spark ideas for happiness in the present and the future. What did you enjoy at school that could bring you more happiness now? What did you enjoy as a teenager that you could enjoy now? What did you enjoy when you first went to work that you could enjoy again now? What did you enjoy as a young adult that you could still enjoy now?

Activity 24
Happy Questions

Action for Happiness Key
Emotion, Trying Out, Direction

Pairs

Rationale

This simple activity is designed to help participants identify activities they will enjoy, and help them have happy thoughts and hence feel happier. It will also generate a happy resource which will be useful to refer to in the future.

Materials

Handout: Finding Happiness through Questions

Process/procedure

1. Form pairs of people.

2. Give participants the list of questions

3. Each pair come up with three answers to each question that would work for both partners e.g. for question one they need to come up with three things that they could both do that they'd both find fun or satisfying.

Plenary/debrief

Collect in one answer from each pair for each question and flip-chart them.

- The list is a resource – how can you use this resource?
- How can you add to this resource?

Notes including comments and variations

Do this activity in trios or fours.

Use the questions as the basis of a resource for keeping a journal. This activity illustrates how powerful questions can be in accessing happiness.

Handout: Finding Happiness through Questions

1. What could you do for an afternoon that you'd find fun or satisfying?
2. What could you do for an hour?
3. What could you do for 15 minutes?
4. What could you plan to do next weekend?
5. What could you do right now, that doesn't need any planning?
6. What can you do that costs money?
7. What can you do that doesn't cost anything?
8. What can you do that will stimulate your mind and get you thinking?
9. What would give you a sense of accomplishment?
10. Which course or evening class would you find interesting?
11. What practical skill would you like to learn?
12. What physical activity would you like to try?
13. If a friend were visiting, what would you suggest you do together?
14. What could you do that would enable you to meet new people?
15. What could you do that would enable you to make new friends?
16. What enjoyable activity could you do on your own?
17. What enjoyable activity could you do as a group – with family, friends or neighbours?
18. What could you do at home?
19. Where would you like to go?
20. What could you do that you've never done before?
21. What have you enjoyed doing in the past?
22. What interesting activities and events are listed in the local paper?
23. Where else could you get ideas of available activities and events?
24. Where else could you look for inspiration? The library? Tourist information? Google?
25. What could you volunteer to do?

Based on © Freeman and Freeman (2012) pp 48-49.

Activity 25
Keeping a Happiness Log

Action for Happiness Key
Meaning, Appreciating, Direction

Individual

Rationale

This activity will enable participants to learn from their own experience about what happiness means to them, as well as to clarify the links between their happiness and their emotions. It can also enable them to create a list of different actions to increase their own happiness.

Materials

Handout : Keeping a Happiness Log

Process/procedure

1. This activity is suitable for homework where there are two parts to a workshop which have a gap between them (e.g. a happiness workshop which takes place on the first Saturday of consecutive months).

2. Use the handout to record your activities and associated level of happiness for 1 week. Make a quick note of one of the things you were doing each hourly period and how happy you were doing it on a 7 point scale.

3. Before the next workshop use your happiness log to answer the following questions:
   - Which activities did you enjoy?
   - Which activities were less enjoyable?
   - Which of the following activities did you enjoy the most:
     - Activities that involved doing things for others/
     - Activities that involved exercising or taking care of your body
     - Activities that involved learning new things
     - Activities that intended to be pleasurable
     - Activities that involved planning or having goals to look forward to
     - Activities that involved connecting with people
     - Activities that involved savouring the world around

Plenary/debrief

- Which activities could you do more of?
- Would it make sense to increase activities involving short-term pleasures?
- What can you do to make the less enjoyable activities more enjoyable?
- Which of the happiness 'keys' are you currently low on? What practical steps can you take? E.g. if you are light on physical activity you could buy a pedometer, go for a brief walk at lunch-time each day or go for a swim each week.

Handout: Keeping a Happiness Log

Time	What was I doing?	How happy was I feeling? (on a scale of 1 to 7)
8.00-9.00 am		
9.00-10.00 am		
10.00-11.00 am		
11.00-12.00 am		
12.00-1.00 pm		
1.00-2.00 pm		
2.00-3.00 pm		
3.00-4.00 pm		
4.00-5.00 pm		
5.00-6.00 pm		
6.00-7.00 pm		
7.00-8.00 pm		
8.00-9.00 pm		
9.00-10.00 pm		

Scale

7 = very happy
6 = quite happy
5 = a little happy
4 = neither happy nor unhappy
3 = a little unhappy
2 = quite unhappy
1 = very unhappy

Activity 26
Happiness Goals

Action for Happiness Key
Direction

Individual

Rationale

This activity focuses on helping participants identify happiness-related goals, and create a list of concrete actions which will contribute to achieving these goals. Since we know that making a public commitment increases our motivation, the activity will also give participants the opportunity to commit by sharing their goals with others.

Materials

None required.

Process/procedure

1. Introduce the activity by saying something along the following lines: Do you dream of being happier? Turn your dreams into goals. Goals are dreams with deadlines. Dreams are the stuff of imagination. Goals recruit action to the realisation of dreams. This activity is about helping your dreams come true.

2. Identify at least one goal for 5 of the 10 Action for Happiness Keys to Happiness.

3. Examples

   - *Relating* Go to the cinema once a month with my best friend.
   - *Exercising*: Spend 30 minutes each day exercising – walking to/from work, using the stairs instead of the lift, walking in the park at lunch-time.
   - *Appreciating*: Spend 10 minutes each day noticing my surroundings and how my body feels.
   - *Trying Out*: Find out how my car works and how to carry out basic maintenance and repairs.
   - *Giving*: Spend one day a month volunteering for my favourite charity.

4. These are high level goals. Now you've selected them, break each down into smaller sub-goals.

5. It is probably too ambitious to work towards all 5 goals at the same time so start with the one or two goals which resonate most with you.

6. Share with another participant what you are going to do to start increasing your happiness. Or, have a happiness cocktail party i.e. each person meets another and each share what they will do to increase their happiness and then move on to another person

Plenary/debrief

- With whom will you share what you are going to do to increase your happiness?
- Remember: public commitment increases motivation.

Activity 27
Measure Your Happiness

Action for Happiness Key
Trying Out, Appreciating, Direction

Individual

Rationale

Some workshop participants will be interested in having a baseline measure of their happiness before they do any activities, in order to understand better where they are now and how the happiness activities they choose to do improve how they think and feel about their lives. There are an increasing number of research-based tools available to measure your level of happiness. The one we have suggested is psychometrically valid and free to use providing you credit the authors of the scale (details provided below).

This activity also provides the opportunity to discuss, as a group, differences in levels of happiness, changes over time (for example, thinking about yourself as a teenager and as an adult), different definitions of happiness (see Chapter 3 for more information) and of course, to learn from each other by sharing ideas for activities which contribute to increasing your level of happiness. This may give participants the opportunity and confidence to consider trying new things as well as to appreciate the many 'ordinary' things which people value highly.

Participants might be interested to know that in research on the happiness level of over 1 million people across 45 nations, the average response is 6.75 on a 10 point scale of happiness (Myers & Diener, 2000).

Materials

Copies of the Flourishing Scale (FS). Permission is granted without charge as long as you credit the authors as follows: Diener, E., Wirtz, D., Tov, W., Kim-Prieto, C., Choi, D., Oishi, S., & Biswas-Diener, R. (2009). New measures of well-being: Flourishing and positive and negative feelings. *Social Indicators Research, 39*, 247-266.

Process/procedure

1. Point out that the aim of the activity is to baseline our happiness, that is, to understand our level of happiness now so that we can see improvements over time, as we engage in different activities.

2. Introduce the questionnaire i.e. explain that it's a short 8-statement measure of self-perceived success in important areas of life such as relationships, self-esteem, purpose, and optimism. The scale provides a single psychological well-being score. The possible range of scores is from 8 (lowest possible) to 56 (highest possible). A high score represents a person with many psychological resources and strengths.

3. Distribute copies of the Flourishing Scale and ask participants to complete it confidentially.

The following steps are optional – see caveat in the Notes below.

4. Each person writes their score anonymously on a slip of paper (voting slip) and passes it to the facilitator.

5. The facilitator compiles a rough histogram of happiness in the room.

Plenary/debrief

Encourage participants to share their observations with partner or with group (if small). For example, is their result as expected? Did anything about it surprise them? How do they think their result has changed over time (for example, thinking about themselves 1-5-10-20 years ago) and why/why not? What do they do currently that contributes to their happiness? Are there any gaps in their responses or anything which stands out (e.g. a lower score for optimism)?

Ask what we can all do to get the most out of this workshop e.g. what attitudes and behaviour will help get the most from this workshop?

If you do the histogram, invite participants to check out where they are on the histogram.
Reiterate that our goal is to move everyone up the happiness scale at least a bit.

Notes including comments and variations

Share with a partner what you will do to increase your level of happiness.

Instead of sharing with a partner, have a happiness cocktail party i.e. each person meets another and each shares what they will do to increase their happiness and then move on to the next person. Feel free to re-use other people's ideas!

Some participants may compare their score with others and feel negative as a result. Encourage people to focus on the small steps that they can personally take to change their level of happiness, and to be curious and experimental: remind people again of the old saying 'if you always do what you always did, you will always get what you always got'.

The Flourishing Scale is also available in Chinese, German, Hungarian, Italian, Norwegian, Filipino and Turkish. See website for further information: internal.psychology.illinois.edu/~ediener/FS.html

Flourishing Scale

©Copyright Ed Diener and Robert Biswas-Diener, January 2009

Below are 8 statements with which you may agree or disagree. Using the 1–7 scale below, indicate your agreement with each item by indicating that response for each statement.

7 - Strongly agree
6 - Agree
5 - Slightly agree
4 - Neither agree nor disagree
3 - Slightly disagree
2 - Disagree
1 - Strongly disagree

_____ I lead a purposeful and meaningful life
_____ My social relationships are supportive and rewarding
_____ I am engaged and interested in my daily activities
_____ I actively contribute to the happiness and well-being of others
_____ I am competent and capable in the activities that are important to me
_____ I am a good person and live a good life
_____ I am optimistic about my future
_____ People respect me

Scoring:

Add the responses, varying from 1 to 7, for all eight items. The possible range of scores is from 8 (lowest possible) to 56 (highest psychological well-being possible). A high score represents a person with many psychological resources and strengths.

Activity 28
Micro Activities

Action for Happiness Key
Trying Out, Direction

Individual

Rationale

The purpose of this activity is to emphasise the first five Action for Happiness keys to happiness and to have participants start turning the keys from ideas into personal actions.

Materials

None required.

Process/procedure

1. What is the smallest thing you can do to increase your happiness? Smile? Stretch?

2. Using the first five 'keys' from Action for Happiness as our starting point (Giving, Relating, Exercising, Appreciating and Trying out), what is the smallest thing you can do to increase your happiness in this workshop?

Here are some examples:
- *Giving* (i.e. doing things for others). Resolve to be as helpful as possible to other participants.
- *Relating*, (i.e. connecting with people). Talk to someone in the coffee break
- *Exercising*, (i.e. taking care of your body). Go for a walk at lunchtime.
- *Appreciating*, (i.e. noticing and valuing the world around). Express your gratitude for someone or something in your life to another participant.
- *Trying out*, (i.e. continuing to learn new things). Hopefully, you're doing this right now.

3. Look for opportunities and ways of doing these when you can during the workshop and keep a note of them, perhaps in your happiness journals.

4. At the end of the day tally up how you've done and what you've observed other people doing.

Plenary/debrief

No debrief is needed for this one. Unless, at the end of the day, you ask people for examples of what they've done based on the first five keys and what they've observed other people doing.

Notes including comments and variations

Brainstorm more examples of what people could do to increase their happiness in this workshop based on each of the first five 'keys' from Action for Happiness.

Activity 29
What's Going Right?

Action for Happiness Key
Emotion, Appreciating

Individual, pairs

Rationale

People often focus most of their attention on what isn't going/hasn't gone/won't go right for them, rather than focussing on what is going/has gone/will go right. Constantly thinking negatively takes its toll. It saps positive energy and positive emotion, and can have a damaging effect on our happiness. In short, in order to be happier we need to practise turning our attention away from the negative things that happen and focus more on what is going well for us.

Materials

None required.

Process/procedure

1. Take a moment to pause and ask yourself 'What is going right for me at this very moment?'

2. Ask everyone to put up their hand and lower it when they've thought of an example of 'one thing that's going right for me right now'.

3. Find a partner and compare examples.

4. Ask each pair to find another pair and share examples.

5. Ask people to call out their examples and write them up on a flip chart.

6. Fix the flip charts to the walls to create a positive atmosphere for the rest of in the workshop.

Plenary/debrief

Ask participants how they are feeling now.

Ask participants when they can use this technique for generating positive thoughts to increase their happiness i.e. in what situations?

Notes including comments and variations

Ask participants to complete the Flourishing Scale (see the Measure your Happiness activity) after doing this activity.

Activity 30
Savour the Moment

Action for Happiness Key
Emotional,
Appreciating

Individual

Rationale

Learning how to savour the good things in life, no matter how small, is a key component of enduring happiness. Focusing on positive things also boosts your mood, and identifying what's good in your life helps you notice more of it.

Materials

None required.

Process/procedure

1. Explain that happiness is a skill and a key element of that is learning how to savour moments: savouring has been defined as 'The capacity to attend to, appreciate and enhance the positive experiences in one's life' (Bryant, F. & Veroff, J. (2007). *Savouring: A new model of positive experience*. Mahwah, NJ: Lawrence Erlbaum Associates). In other words, savouring is about something you *do*, not something that happens to you, so it requires you to be actively engaged in the process.

2. Ask yourself, *'what is going right for me right now?'* Take your time to reflect on this question; perhaps it is something about your physical surroundings, your health, what you have achieved today or even something you are looking forward to happening later today. For example:
   - Sitting by the fireside on a cold winter's day
   - Feeling relaxed after a good night's sleep
   - Got some work done this morning
   - Looking forward to a luxurious bubblebath

3. Collect and write up about five or six examples from participants.

4. Ask participants to select one example and really savour it, i.e. slow down, take time to notice it using all your senses, delight in the experience of it and make the pleasure last. So there are four elements to savouring:

   - Take your time, don't rush
   - Pay attention to what you are doing & use all your senses
   - Really enjoy it, delight in it and allow yourself to accept the pleasure it can give
   - Extend the pleasure of that experience i.e. make it last by reflecting on it.

Plenary/debrief

- What else in your life can you savour?
- When in your life can you do that?

Activity 31
Appreciation and Gratitude for This Day

Action for Happiness Key
Appreciating

Individual

Rationale

Expressing gratitude or appreciation in life makes a significant contribution to enduring happiness. In fact, gratitude is so important to us that it has been identified as one of the 24 universal character strengths, recognised by many different cultures and societies across the globe.

Materials

Handout: Appreciation

Process/procedure

1. Make a brief note of all the positive things (no matter how small) that have happened to you so far today i.e. since the day started at 12 am this morning. For example, you slept well, woke on time, had a refreshing shower, got rid of uggy taste in mouth by cleaning your teeth.

2. As a group brainstorm 'all the positive things that have happened to us today since the day started at 12 am'. Collect about 25 things in the brainstorm.

3. Ask the participants to make a list of things that apply to them personally and how it made them feel. Use the proforma provided for the purpose. Distribute copies of the proforma to everyone.

4. Share results with a partner.

Plenary/debrief

- Who had more than ten items? Who had more than seven? Who had more than five?

- Who is surprised by how much they have to appreciate and feel grateful for so far today at X o'clock this morning?

- How can you use this experience to enhance your feelings of appreciation in the future?

Handout: Appreciation

What I Appreciated	How did I feel?

Example:

What I appreciated	How did I feel?
A long lie in followed by breakfast in bed and the Sunday newspaper	Very relaxed, upbeat and looking forward to the rest of the day
Being invited to lunch with friends at a new bistro in town	Pleased to be included! We had a great chat about life, love and everything. I enjoyed the food and the prices pleased my wallet too!
A long walk on the downs with my family and our dog Sasha	It was great to be outside all together, walking and talking and getting some fresh air and exercise. I felt really invigorated. I love playing hide and seek with the kids and it was fun trying to teach Sasha some new tricks.
Communal cooking	When we got back from the walk we decided to cook our evening meal together, using what we had in the cupboards. It was a real adventure, and great fun and the result was, well, interesting! Our 5 year old made honey and ham sandwiches for starters.
Sitting in front of the fire with my wife after the kids had gone to bed, just chatting	I relished the quiet time we had just to chat and make plans. I was glad the day went well, that the kids had fun and I feel ready for the week ahead.

Activity 32
Optimism – Best Possible Self

Action for Happiness Key
Emotion, Direction, Appreciating

Individual

Rationale

Research suggests that optimistic thinking enhances happiness firstly because if you are optimistic about your goals you will put time and effort into reaching them; perseverance and motivation mean you're more likely to reach your goals and overcome obstacles than if you don't persevere and aren't motivated. Secondly optimistic thinking boosts your mood and your morale; having a bright future ahead of you, or simply having something to look forward to, makes you feel full of energy and enthusiasm. It's a kind of virtuous circle. This activity shows participants a simple way of strengthening the optimism 'muscle' by writing about their best possible future self.

Materials

Happiness journals or pen and paper for notes.

Process/procedure

1. Introduce the activity by explaining the connection between optimism and happiness.

2. Ask participants to sit quietly.

3. Spend about 10-15 minutes writing in your happiness journal about how you see yourself in a few years time when all your current hopes, dreams and goals have all been realised….Visualise a future life where everything has turned out the way you wanted….. It may be one, five or ten years' time….. Imagine that during this time you have worked hard and achieved all your goals….. What would your life be like? Describe in writing what you imagine…… It may be that you are happily married or settled with a partner and have close family and friends around you….. Perhaps you are doing the job you have always dreamed of….you may be retired and spending all your time on your lifelong hobby….maybe you have moved to another country….what can you see?....who are you with…what are you doing?

4. Find a partner and share the parts you feel comfortable sharing with that partner (5 minutes each way).

Plenary/debrief

- Who found they had something or some things in common with their partner?

- What can you do to realise some parts of these aspirations (dreams)?

Let the participants know that in the research referred to above, people were invited to continue to write about their best possible future selves as often and for as long as they wanted to over the course of four weeks, so remind participants to re-do this exercise. Writing it down is important because it helps you organise your thoughts and gives you the opportunity to learn about yourself and what is important to you.

Notes including comments and variations

Instead of 'best possible future self' the focus can be shifted to 'best possible outcomes'. In this form it can be used as a tool for visualisation and achieving desired goals.

Another visualisation is to focus on particular situation or contexts in life. For example, the core instruction might be to 'spend 10-15 minutes writing in your happiness journal about how your see yourself at work in a few years time when all your current goals have been realised - you might be in the same job or a different job, with the same employer or a different employer' etc.

Do this activity (with appropriate modification) immediately after the 'What's going right' activity.

Suggest to the participants that every week or so they reread what they've written and edit it, deleting or changing it. This will keep it fresh in their minds and help them move towards their best possible selves.

Activity 33
Music Playlists

Action for Happiness Key
Emotion, Appreciating, Meaning

Group, brainstorming

Rationale

We all know that music has a remarkable power to change our mood very quickly, and that includes making us feel happier and more upbeat. By pooling our resources this activity gives us the opportunity to compile our own personal playlist of songs which will lift our mood.

Materials

None required.

Process/procedure

1. Introduction: Sometimes music gives us a lift so it would be good to have to hand a ready-made playlist of 'songs of happiness'.

The mental health charity 'Mind' did a survey to find people's happy songs. The top three were:
- 'Let me entertain you' by Robbie Williams
- 'Walking on sunshine' by Katrina and the Waves
- 'Shiny, happy people' by REM

Now is our chance to pool our knowledge of happy songs to produce our own list – which we can do by brainstorming.

2. Facilitate a brainstorm on the topic: 'What songs make me feel happy?'

3. Ask people to (1) make a note of any they don't know to check out later, and (2) pick out three songs to make a start on compiling their own playlist of mood-lifting songs.

Plenary/debrief

None required.

Notes including comments and variations

Sometimes we want different playlists to access different types of happiness e.g. vitality and energy rather than say, serenity and calm. The top three songs for *relaxation* in the Mind survey were:
- 'Thank you' by Dido
- 'Bridge over troubled water' by Simon and Garfunkel
- 'Porcelain' by Moby.

Once again you can brainstorm more relaxing songs and then invite participants to (1) make a note of any they don't know to check out later, and (2) pick out three songs to make a start on compiling a playlist of mood-lifting songs.

Activity 34
Chucklebelly

Action for Happiness Key
__Emotion__

Group

Rationale

Laughter is beneficial in many ways, both physical and mental. It can help:
- boost the immune and circulatory systems
- enhance oxygen intake
- relax muscles throughout the entire body
- trigger the natural release of endorphins, relieves pain
- lowers and stabilizes blood pressure
- improve alertness and creativity
- promotes sound sleep
- promotes an overall sense of well-being.

Materials

None required.

Process/procedure

Clear a large area of space on the floor, enough to accommodate all the people who will be playing. Ask one person to lie down on the floor. Ask a second person to lie down placing their head on the first person's stomach. Person number three lies down placing their head on number two's tummy etc. Once everyone is in place, ask for silence and wait to see how long before the giggles begin.

Plenary/debrief

None required.

Notes including comments and variations

Variation: begin the same way, only instead of being quiet, each person has to take turns saying "giggle guts" or some other silly word or phrase. If you have a large group, you can remove people if they are the first to laugh and keep playing until you have a "winner".

Variation: begin the same way, only instead of being quiet, the first person says "Ha!" the second person "HaHa", third "HaHaHa" etc.. The idea is to get through everyone in the group saying "ha" the number of times as their number without actually laughing.

Activity 35
Relaxation - Progressive Muscle Relaxation

Action for Happiness Key
Emotion, Appreciating

Individual

Rationale

Since mind and body are interconnected, being able to relax your body means that your mind is more likely to become more peaceful and calm too. This exercise gives participants the chance to practice a method that they can use in their everyday lives to release tension, stress and anxiety. In addition this is a great activity to do as a preliminary to visualisation exercises because it allows you to gain more control over your thinking and your imagination.

Materials

None required.

Process/procedure

1. Introduce the activity along the following lines: Anxious thoughts (rumination) and stress produce anxious feelings which are reflected in our bodies. For example, our breathing tends to be more shallow and quicker, our hearts beat faster and our muscles become tighter. An American doctor, Edmund Jacobson (1888-1983) discovered a method for relaxing physical tension which had the effect of also calming thoughts and feelings. In his words: "An anxious mind cannot exist in a relaxed body." So he looked for a way of relaxing the body and came up with a method that he called 'progressive muscle relaxation'. It's based on the observation that people are not always aware if they have tense muscles, people are able to consciously tense muscles and most people find it easier to relax a muscle after they have consciously tensed it. Relaxing a muscle simply means not tensing it. So progressive muscle relaxation involves simply tensing and then relaxing each group of the muscles around the body in turn.

2. Make yourself comfortable. You might want to loosen your clothes. You might want to take off your shoes. You might want to sit in a chair. You might want to lie on the floor. Just do what you need to do to get comfortable.

3. Close your eyes and spend a minute or two becoming more aware of your breathing. As you do so, your breathing will probably gradually slow down a little and become deeper. And you'll probably feel your body starting to relax a little.

4. Now become aware of your feet. Press down on the floor and tense your toes. Hold this for about five seconds and then release the muscles in your feet into a relaxed state for about ten seconds. Enjoy the fact that the muscles in your feet are no longer tensed.

5. Now move your attention to your legs and tense your calf and thigh muscles and count slowly to five and then release into a relaxed state and slowly count to ten. Enjoy the freedom from tension in the legs.

6. Next move your attention to your hips area including the muscles around your hips and buttocks. Tense these muscles for five seconds and then release and relax for ten seconds enjoying the freedom

from tension in these muscles.

7. Proceed the same way around the main groups of muscles in your body:
- Stomach
- Chest
- Hands and arms
- Shoulders and neck
- Face, including mouth and tongue.

8. When you've completed this then savour the thought that you've checked all your major muscle groups and you now know that you've relaxed the tension in each one. Enjoy the feeling of release from tension. Focus your attention again on your breathing and breathe slowly and deeply into your whole body and into each of the muscle groups in your body. Savour the feeling of release and relaxation. Take time to enjoy your body free of tension.

Plenary/debrief
- How does your body feel now?
- Have your thoughts slowed?
- When could you use this method in your life after this workshop?

Notes including comments and variations

Let participants know they don't have to do this perfectly. It works even if they do it in a half-hearted way. So long as they move around their body and cover a good range of muscle groups it will produce a more relaxed state.

Activity 36
Relaxation - Basic Visualisation

Action for Happiness Key
Emotion

Individual

Rationale

It's not easy to be happy if your mind is frequently full of anxious, negative thoughts and your body is frequently full of tension and stress. This exercise works by enlisting your imagination in the service of relaxation, both mental and physical, and in doing so contributes to your happiness.

Materials

Relaxing music.

Process/procedure

1. Ask the participants to make themselves as comfortable as they can e.g. sitting comfortably or lying on the floor.

2. Ask participants to become aware of their breathing. Allow it to slow down and become a little deeper.

3. Ask the participants to imagine a relaxing place or scene, such as a meadow with a nearby trickling stream, a perfect beach or a wonderful mountainside. Put on some relaxing music and dim the lights.

4. Ask the participants to imagine that they are there right now.
   "Allow yourself to become part of this relaxing environment... Focus on how it feels... Notice the beautiful scenery with its colours, and any relaxing sounds and any sweet fragrances.... Allow yourself to drift away from this room and fully immerse yourself in this relaxing environment created by your own imagination.... Savour the relaxation and pleasure of just being there..." and so on.

Plenary/debrief

- Where did you go?
- How did it feel?
- How can you access that state of relaxation when you want to in your life?

Activity 37
Raisin Meditation

Action for Happiness Key
Appreciating

Individual

Rationale

Often, our anxiety, unhappiness or stress results from our thoughts about the past or the future and we are so wrapped up in our thoughts that we forget to live in the present. Research shows that the practice of mindfulness - which is defined by Jon Kabat-Zinn (2006) as paying attention in a particular way: on purpose, in the present moment and non-judgementally - contributes to increased happiness and reduced stress, anxiety and depressive symptoms.

This activity provides a simple way to start your mindfulness practice if it's not something you have come across before. Mindfulness is all about cultivating awareness of the here-and-now and learning to notice what is going on for you physically and mentally, without judgement. There are numerous ways to practice mindfulness - in this activity we use an edible object because it provides the opportunity to start noticing using all your senses.

Materials

A bag of raisins

Process/procedure

1. Introduce the activity by reference to the rationale (above).

2. Hand round the bag of raisins and invite each participant to take one.

3. Provide the following instruction:

> *Start by picking up your raisin and exploring how it feels in our fingers. How does it feel as it makes contact with your skin? Notice its weight and texture.*
>
> *Next, concentrate your attention on how it looks. Examine each detail, each crinkle and fold.*
>
> *Then lift the raisin to your nose and notice how it smells.*
>
> *Now put the raisin to your tongue, let it sit there long enough to notice its texture. Then explore the raisin with your tongue without biting it.*
>
> *Now start to chew the raisin slowly concentrating on its change in texture as you do so. Is it soft? Hard? Rough? Smooth? Notice the taste. Is there any difference in the taste in different parts of your mouth? Is the taste in the front of your mouth different from the taste in the back?*
>
> *Next, gradually and slowly, swallow the raisin. Notice as much as you can of the detail of that process.*

Finally, think about what it feels like to have swallowed the raisin. Does any taste remain in your mouth? Does any of its scent remain? What remaining sensations are there on your tongue, in your mouth and around your teeth?

Plenary/debrief

Ask a participant to describe the experience. How did it differ to your normal style of eating? What did you make of that experience?

How does that experience relate to mindfulness? (ensure a connection is made to the practice of noticing what is going on in the present, and in doing so, freedom from thoughts which worry us or make us feel unhappy).

What might it be like to notice every detail of the things we tend to do on autopilot, like tying your shoelaces or brushing our teeth?

Notes including comments and variations

This activity can be done with virtually anything. Instead of raisin use a square of chocolate or a piece of fruit, a nut, a pretzel or some other dried fruit such as dried mango.

Activity 38
Smiles Cocktail Party

Action for Happiness Key
__Emotion, Relating__

Pairs, small groups

Rationale

Just as the way we think can affect the way we feel and behave, so can the way we behave affect how we feel and think. Recent scientific research suggests that it's possible to feel certain emotions just by adopting the corresponding facial expression (Soussignan, 2002). Frowning can make you feel negative, and smiling can make you feel happier. This activity gives participants the opportunity to smile, even if they don't much feel like it, to see for themselves how it can lighten their mood.

Materials

None required.

Process/procedure

1. Introduce the activity by referring to the rationale above and pointing out that we can lower our mood by just pretending to frown and raise our mood by putting on a pretend smile i.e. by acting happy.

2. Start a cocktail party where instead of conversation we simply go round spending a minute with each other giving each other a smile, making it as heartfelt as we can, but simply acting it if we can't.

Plenary/debrief

What did you do to make yourself smile? (E.g. I find it helps if I say to myself 'I really like this person')

Notes including comments and variations

As you meet each person, say to yourself internally '*I really like this person.*'

As you meet each person say to yourself internally the words:
- May you be safe
- May you be healthy
- May you be live with peace
- May you be happy

The mantra above can be changed to something that is particularly suitable to your participants.

Activity 39
Faking It 1 – Method Acting

Action for Happiness Key
Emotion, Trying Out, Relating

Pairs, small groups

Rationale

This exercise is an extension of the previous one (Smiles Cocktail Party) in which participants are encouraged to smile at others even if they don't feel much like smiling. This activity gives participants the opportunity to experiment with method acting other positive emotions of their choice, to see how it affects the way they feel.

Materials

None required.

Process/procedure

1. Introduce this activity in term of its rationale, above.

2. Ask participants to act out (in a 'method acting' way) a cocktail party in which each person takes on the role of someone expressing one of the following emotions:
    - Joyful
    - Serene
    - Proud
    - In love
    - etc

3. After 2 minutes ask each participant to switch to one of the other emotions. Repeat after 2 more minutes.

Plenary/debrief

- Did you manage to get into role and if so how?
- Which emotion felt best?
- How can you use this in your everyday life?

Activity 40
Faking It 2 – Postures

Action for Happiness Key
Emotion, Trying Out, Relating

Individual

Rationale

Research has shown that adopting the posture of a particular emotion helps to generate that emotion. In other words, our body language and the way we behave affect our thinking and our feelings (as well as the other way round). For example, 'faking' a body posture of competence or power (such as the 'arms held aloft' pose adopted by winning athletes) can help us feel that way and we can use this to help us cope better in stressful situations. In this activity participants have the opportunity to experiment with different body postures to see the impact on mood.

Materials

None required

Process/procedure

1. Introduce this activity in term of its rationale, above.

2. Ask the participants to adopt a posture that for them expresses victory or achievement. They can also adopt the appropriate facial expression.

3. Then ask them to adopt the following in turn (allowing a reasonable time for participants to get in role):
   - Adopt a posture that for them expresses confidence
   - Adopt a posture that for them expresses compassion
   - Adopt a posture that for them expresses joy
   - Adopt a posture that for them expresses an open heart

Plenary/debrief

- Which was hardest?
- Which was easiest?
- Which felt best?
- How can you use this experience in your life outside this workshop?

Notes including comments and variations

As a group, brainstorm more positive emotions first and add them to the list or vary the ones given.

Activity 41
Some Facts About Happiness

Action for Happiness Key
Trying Out

Individual, pairs

Rationale

A great deal of new academic research has been carried out in the past 15 years since positive psychology first appeared as a science-based academic discipline. That means that there is a huge amount of new knowledge about happiness, some of which participants may be unaware. Fortunately many of the research findings have been condensed into easy-to-read books written by the researchers themselves (see the end of this book for details of some of them).

This activity is designed to convey some of the facts about happiness as they currently stand, and to help participants reflect on the significance of some of the new knowledge about happiness for their personal lives and for social policy.

Materials

Handout: Some Facts about Happiness

Process/procedure

1. Introduce this activity by talking about the growth in evidence-based knowledge about happiness over the last 2 decades.

2. Distribute the handout: 'Some Facts about Happiness'.

3. Ask participants to tick the three facts about happiness that they see as most significant.

4. Then ask the participants to rank their three in order of significance.

5. Ask participants to find a partner and compare what they have each come up with and then spend five minutes exploring the reasons for any differences.

6. Do a 'round robin' to collect what each person has rated the three most significant facts, if the workshop number is small e.g. below 25. And if the workshop number is large (e.g. over 25) then collect in the topmost significant fact from each person. Use this to create a rough histogram on a flip-chart.

Plenary/debrief

Ask for observations, comments or reflections on the resulting histogram.
- If you were the prime minister which of the facts to do you think would seem most important to you ... and why?
- Do any of these facts have any implications for what you might do in your life or any implications for government or society generally?

Handout: Some Facts about Happiness

1. The world's richest countries have more than doubled their material standard of living in the last 50 years but there has been no significant rise in recorded happiness in these countries. (*Source: R. Layard, Happiness, 2011, second edition, p32*)

2. The poorest people become happier with increasing wealth but the effect of wealth in raising happiness rapidly declines as income rises. (*Source: Helliwell, J., Layard, R. and Sachs, J. World Happiness Report, Columbia University: Earth Institute, 2012*)

3. Helping other people contributes to your happiness (i.e. doing good makes you feel good). When people do good, their brain becomes active in the same reward centre as when they experience other rewards. (*Source: S. Lyubomirsky, The How of Happiness, 2007; J. Rilling et al, Neuron, 35:395-405, 2002, E. Dunn et al, Science, 319:1687-8, 2008*)

4. Empathy is part of human nature. If a friend is given an electric shock, it hurts us in the same part of our brain as if we ourselves are given an electric shock. (*Source: Singer, T., Seymour, B., O'Doherty, J., Kaube, H., Dolan, R. & Frith, C. (2004). Empathy for pain involves the affective but not sensory components of pain. Science. 303:1157–61*)

5. Happiness is contagious. So one way of contributing to the happiness of your friends, your family and others you love is to become happier yourself. Research shows that the happiness of a close contact increases the your chance of being happy by 15%. The happiness of a 2nd-degree contact (e.g. friend's spouse) increases it by 10% and the happiness of a 3rd-degree contact (e.g. friend of a friend of a friend) by 6%. (*Source: Fowler, J.H. & Christakis, N.A. (2008). British Medical Journal, 337:a2338*)

6. Happier people tend to live longer. Happiness reduces the likelihood of falling ill. Positive emotions reduce stress and excessive or chronic stress can cause heart disease and other health problems. The effect of happiness on longevity in healthy populations is remarkably strong. The size of the effect is comparable to that of not smoking (*Source: Veenhoven, R. (2008). Healthy happiness: effects of happiness on physical. Journal of Happiness Studies, 9 (3): 449-469*)

7. Being happier helps us function better i.e. become more energetic, creative, resilient and productive (*Source: Ryan, R. & Deci, E. (2001). On happiness and human potentials: A review of research on hedonic and eudaimonic well-being In S. Fiske (Ed.), Annual review of psychology, Vol. 52, pp. 141-166*).

8. We can learn to be happier and our happiness can be permanently altered. Surveys show that long periods of unhappiness are followed by long periods of happiness. (*Source: Headey, B. et al. (2010)*)

9. External circumstances (such as wealth, marital status, nationality and gender) only explain about 10% of the variation in happiness between people. (*Source: Lyubomirsky, S. (2007). The How of Happiness*)

10. About 40 per cent of the variation in happiness between people can be explained by 'lifestyle' factors (e.g. whether we take exercise) and choices about our actions and our thoughts - importantly, these are factors that people have much control over. (*Source: Lyubomirsky, S. (2007). The How of Happiness*)

11. People tend to become happier as they move from middle age into old age. Happiness follows a U shape across the lifecycle. On average we're happier when young and old and least happy in middle age. (*Source: Oswald, A. & Blanchflower, D. (2008). Is well-being U-shaped over the life cycle? Social Science & Medicine, 66(6), 1733-1749*)

12. Money spent on 'experiences' (especially new experiences) tends to yield more happiness than the

equivalent amount of money spent on 'goods' (...so perhaps 'goods' aren't quite so 'good' after all). *(Source: Van Boven, L. & Gilovich, T. (2003). 'To Do or to Have? That Is the Question', Journal of Personality and Social Psychology, 85(6), 1193-1202)*

13. People who take regular exercise are happier than those who don't. *(Source: De Moor, M. M., Boomsma, D.I., Stubbe, J.H., Willemsen, G.& de Geus, E.C. (2008). Testing Causality in the Association Between Regular Exercise and Symptoms of Anxiety and Depression. Arch Gen Psych, 65(8), 897-905)*

14. People who meditate tend to be happier than people who don't. People who did eight sessions of mindfulness meditation training were on average 20% happier one month later than a control group and had better responses in their immune system. Such training can lead to structural brain changes including increased grey-matter density in the hippocampus, known to be important for learning and memory, and in structures associated with self-awareness, compassion and introspection. *(Source: Davidson, R. et al. (2003).Alterations in brain and immune function produced by mindfulness meditation. Psychosomatic Medicine. 65, 564-70. Hölzel, B.K. et al. (2011). Mindfulness practice leads to increases in regional brain gray matter density. Psychiatry Research: Neuroimaging. 191(1), 36-43)*

15. We're not very good at predicting what will make us happy (...or remembering what has made us happy). *(Source: Gilbert, D (2007) Stumbling on Happiness. New York: Random House)*

16. The measurement of happiness from self-report correlates well with neuroscientific objective measures of brain activity and third party assessment. It also correlates well with factors that would be expected to impact on happiness such as a bereavement, unemployment, quitting your job and the end of a marriage. This provides confidence in self-report as a valid and reliable measure of happiness. *(Source: Davidson, R. J. (2000). Affective style, psychopathology, and resilience: Brain mechanisms and plasticity, American Psychologist. 55, 1196-1214.)*

17. Economists assume that more choice contributes to our well-being but in fact more choice can diminish our happiness. Research has shown that more choice doesn't necessarily mean better choices or more happiness or satisfaction with choices. *(Source: Schwartz, B. (2004). The Paradox of Choice. New York: Harper Collins)*

18. Studies of Olympic athletes have found that winners of bronze medals are happier than winners of silver medals. One likely explanation is that silver medal winners compare themselves upwards with gold medal winners whereas bronze medal winners compare themselves downwards with those who failed to win any medal. *(Source: Medvec, V., Madey, S. & Gilovich, T. (1995). When less is more: Counterfactual thinking and satisfaction among Olympic medallists. Journal of Personality and Social Psychology. 69(4), 603-610)*

19. What makes us happy is not just less of what makes us unhappy. Happiness is associated with higher levels of activity in the left prefrontal cortex whereas unhappiness is associated with higher levels of activity in the right prefrontal cortex. Even the chemicals are different. The main chemicals associated with happiness (including dopamine, serotonin, oxytocin and endorphins) are different from those associated with anxiety, stress, fear and unhappiness more generally (in particular, cortisol) *(Source: Layard, R. (2005). Happiness: Lessons from a new science. London: Penguin Books)*

20. Studying happiness might contribute to happiness. Although it is not a scientifically established fact the founder of positive psychology, Martin Seligman has claimed that: "Positive psychology makes people happier. Teaching positive psychology, researching positive psychology, using positive psychology ... just reading about positive psychology all make people happier. The people who work in positive psychology are the people with the highest well-being I have ever known. *(Source: Seligman, M. (2011). Flourish. London: Nicholas Brealey Publishing.*

Activity 42
Reasons to be Happy

Action for Happiness Key
Trying Out, Direction

Individual, pairs

Rationale

Being clear about your goals and why you are pursuing them can strengthen your motivation and make it more likely that you'll be successful in achieving your goals. The pursuit of happiness is no different. It's a great strength to be clear about your reasons for taking steps to become happier. Doing what it takes to create more happiness in your life is not always easy and it helps to maintain your motivation by reminding yourself why you are doing this. The process for this activity is the same as for the previous activity, 'Some Facts about Happiness'.

Materials

Handout: Reasons to be Happy.

Process/procedure

1. Introduce this activity in terms of the rationale above.

2. Distribute the handout: 'Reasons to be Happy'.

3. Ask participants to tick or highlight the three benefits of being happier that they value most highly.

4. Then ask the participants to rank those three in the order of importance to them.

5. Ask participants to find a partner and compare what they have each come up with and then spend five minutes exploring any differences and possible reasons for them.

6. Do a 'round robin' to collect what each person has rated the most significant benefits, if the workshop number is small e.g. below 25. And if the workshop number is larger then collect in the topmost benefit from each person. Use this to create a crude histogram on a flip chart.

Plenary/debrief

- Ask for observations, comments or reflections on the resulting histogram. Were there any surprises?
- How different was your choice of three top benefits from those chosen by others?
- What have you learnt about what is most important to you in your goals of becoming happier?

Handout: Reasons to be Happy

Why do you want to be happier? For many people this is a simple question because they see happiness as the ultimate goal. A good example is Richard Layard who wrote the best-selling book Happiness – Lessons from a New Science, which was one of the first books to popularise some of the new research on happiness. For Layard, the greatest happiness is simply the final goal and all other goals are instrumental because they are a means to that end. This is also the position taken by Action for Happiness. According to its website:

There are many things in life that matter to us – including health, freedom, autonomy and achievement. But if we ask why they matter we can generally give further answers – for example, that they make people feel better or more able to enjoy their lives. But if we ask why it matters if people feel better, we can give no further answer. It is self-evidently desirable. Our overall happiness – how we feel about our lives – is what matters to us most. (Action for Happiness Website: http://www.actionforhappiness.org/why-happiness accessed on 22/10/2012)

Other people don't place happiness on quite such a high pedestal. They place high value on other things such as engagement with life, achievement, relationships and meaning in life. For example, Martin Seligman, one of the founding figures in positive psychology and the author of *Authentic Happiness*, has recently argued for a broader concept of human flourishing, writing that "*I (now) disagree with the idea that happiness is the be-all and end-all of well-being and its best measure.*" (Seligman, 2011, p. 25).

We believe that engagement, achievement, relationships and meaning in life all contribute to happiness. Moreover, the happier you are the more likely you are to engage more fully with life, achieve more, enjoy better relationships and find more meaning and purpose in life (see below). There seems to be a number of virtuous circles here with happiness both enhanced by, and contributing to, engagement, achievement, relationships and meaning in life. So it's not surprising that these other potential goals in life play significant parts in the pages of this book.

For us, the bottom line is that it is reasonable to believe that almost everyone would prefer to feel better than worse. Psychologists refer to 'subjective well-being', 'positive affect' and 'flourishing'. In this book we'll just use the term 'happiness' and, as we have seen, for many people that is an end in itself. There are however other reasons to pursue greater happiness. Here are 21 of them. We recommend that you place a tick against any of these reasons that apply to you:

1. Happier people are healthier. The link between happiness and health is evident in many studies. A review of over 160 studies found "clear and compelling" evidence that, other things being equal, happy people experience better health than their unhappy peers (Diener and Chan, 2011).

2. Happy people cope better with illness. There is clear evidence that positive emotions help people to cope with illness. For example, research by Laura Kubzansky et al (2001) followed 1,300 men in their 60s over a 10-year period, and found that the more optimistic men were about half as likely to develop heart disease than the more pessimistic men. They also found that the more optimistic men had a slower rate of pulmonary function decline over a 7-year period.

3. Happier people live longer. Since happier people are healthier and cope better with illness it probably comes as no great surprise that they live longer. Happiness reduces the likelihood of falling ill. This can cause heart disease and other health problems. The effect of happiness on longevity in healthy populations is remarkably strong. The size of the effect is comparable to that of not smoking (Veenhoven, 2008).

4. Being happy is likely to make you look better and fitter. Other things being equal, would you rather look at a happy person or an unhappy person? Being happy will put a smile on your face and we tend to find smiling faces attractive. You'll be more likely to take exercise; when we are feeling unhappy and 'down' we usually don't like taking exercise or doing anything else very energetic. By contrast, when we feel happy and 'up' we're more likely to be motivated to take exercise which will make us fitter and look better. Also, if you are unhappy, you're more likely to in indulge in comfort eating and comfort foods tend to be those loaded with simple carbohydrates like white sugar, which are likely to make you larger than you want to be as well as less fit.

5. Happier people have more friends and closer friends. Evidence for this was provided by Richard Tunney of the University of Nottingham who asked 1760 people a series of questions about their friendships and how happy they were in life. This is not too surprising, really, as happy people are more fun to be around, happier people are more popular and they are more likely to be in a stable romantic relationship with a partner.

6. Happier people are better at solving problems. Research shows that people who are in a good mood solve problems better more easily. They concentrate better are more persistent and are more creative. Whereas negative emotions produces chemicals that trigger the 'flight-or-fight' response, positive emotion produces chemicals that spur us on to look for creative win-win solutions (Fredrickson, 2009).

7. Happier people are more resilient. They have more inner strength. It is also the case that more resilient people are happier, so building resilience offers one pathway to greater happiness (Fredrickson, 2009). This is another of those virtuous circles.

8. Happiness increases self-confidence. "When asked if they'd like to be more confident most people say 'yes!' Confidence is seen as a highly desirable quality, the lack of which prevents you achieving the things you want in life." (Grenville-Jones et al., 2008, p 38).

9. Happier people have more energy and vitality. They live life more actively and they do more.

10. Happy employees are more productive. Since happy people are more resilient and have more vitality and energy and are better at problem-solving its probably not surprising that they are more productive. Actually, happy people function better and outperform unhappy people on almost any measure.

11. Happier people are more successful. As happier people are more resilient, are better at solving problems, have more energy and vitality, are more self-confident and are more productive it probably comes as no surprise that they are more successful. (Lyubomirsky et al, 2005)

12. Happier people learn more. Becoming happier improves concentration, inventiveness and ability to remember things.

13. Happy people earn more. If happy people are more productive, learn more and are more successful it is reasonable to believe that they will earn more – which, unsurprisingly does seem to be the case.

14. Happiness supports the realisation of human potential. Once again, this is not surprising since they function better on almost any measure and they learn more (Ryan and Deci, 2001).

15. Happier people are kinder. There is a strong relationship between feeling good and doing good. According to research, happier people are more likely to share their good fortune with others (Lyubomirsky, 2007). Happy people are more generous with their time and with their money. Happier people make the world a nicer place and a better place.

16. Happiness is good for your loved ones. Happiness is contagious. If you are happier it will help to make those you love happier, especially your family and your friends (Fowler, J. & Christakis, N. 2010).

For parents, being happy benefits your children. Almost all parents want their children to be happy. Parents are role-models for their children. Children can learn to be happier by witnessing the lives of happy parents. In other words, being happy will enhance the happiness of the people you care most about.

17. Happy people are less likely to become depressed   A survey analysis of the result of 51 interventions (involving 4,266 individuals) found that techniques for increasing happiness significantly decreased depressive symptoms (Sin & Lyubomirsky, 2009).

18. The pursuit of happiness and contributing to the total happiness of in the world can offer a solution to the problem of existential angst. According to evolutionary biologists, living organisms are survival machines for their genes with the prime directive to 'go forth and multiply'. In order to go forth and multiply, human beings, like any other mammalian gene-machines, had to solve a problem with three parts: (1) survival to at least child-bearing age, (2) reproduction and (3) ensuring that offspring reached at least child-bearing age.

In the developed world, humans have now solved all three parts of that problem:
(1) The large majority of humans now survive to reach biological old age, i.e. well-past child-bearing age, (2) we nearly all now choose how many children we will bear, (3) we can now be confident that nearly all our children will survive to at least child-bearing age.

Having largely solved this tripartite problem, humans are left contemplating the meaning of life and the purpose of their own particular existence. For most humans in earlier generations, the large majority would have been too busy ensuring they and their families had enough to eat, avoiding disease and injury and avoiding predation by other animals and slaughter or subjugation by other humans.

Those humans who cannot find some other meaning and purpose for their lives are likely to suffer existential angst. Victor Frankl, has argued powerfully that having a sense of meaning, purpose or mission in life is essential for healthy human functioning (Frankl, 2006). He went on to conclude that the main reason for psychological distress in modern life is the absence of purpose as people experienced lives without meaning. Empirical research in recent decades has offered considerable support for Frankl's position. People who find meaning and purpose in the pursuit of happiness by contributing to the total happiness in the world can use this to escape the problem of existential angst.

19. A happier world is good for world peace. Human history is littered with wars. Why is this? Many would argue that it's the human propensity for greed, envy and avarice, which are all pretty unhappy states. Marxists, with their materialist conception of history, would argue that it is the result of the desire by ruling elites to acquire more material possessions i.e. more 'stuff'. Happiness research has, however, found that such external acquisition contributes less than 10 % of human happiness. A world focused on increasing happiness rather than increasing material possessions would be a more peaceful world.

20. Happiness may save the planet.   So long as we persist in the pursuit of maximum material possessions we will make increasing demands on our planet and its environment. We now know that beyond a relatively modest level of material well-being further additions to our material possessions have a negligible effect on our subjective well-being. By pursuing maximum happiness rather than maximum material possessions we can end the increasingly damaging demands on our planet and its environment. There is thus a strong environmental reason for making happiness our goal.

21. It's what most people want. In almost every nation people put happiness in top place when they are asked what they want most out of life (Diener, 2000).

Activity 43
Rip it Up!

Action for Happiness Key
__Trying Out, Direction__

Individual, groups

Rationale

This activity is focussed on simply conveying knowledge about happiness and what it is and isn't, and allowing participants to choose the tips about living happier lives which are most meaningful to them.

Materials

The book entitled *'Greater Happiness: 333 Tips for Living Happier Lives'* (Bourner, O'Hara & Stephens, in press).

Process/procedure

1. Display the book: *'Greater Happiness: 333 Tips for Living Happier Lives'*

2. Tear the book up into roughly equal parts depending on the number of participants e.g. if there are 10 participants then each gets about three sections and if there are 30 participants then each gets one section.

3. Allow the participants 10 minutes to skim-read the section they've got focusing on the tips themselves and then decide on the tip that has most potential for them.

4. Participants each call out the tip they see as most valuable/helpful to them – which the facilitator flip-charts.

5. Then do an NGT (nominal group technique) on the tips that have been flip-charted (see the appendix for how to do an NGT).

Plenary/debrief

- How did you feel when the book was torn up?
- How can you use the top three tips from the NGT process in your life?

Activity 44
Pub Quiz on Happiness

Action for Happiness Key
Appreciating, Trying Out

Small groups

Rationale

This activity is a great energiser if used at an early stage in your workshop. It's also a great way of conveying a lot of information about happiness in an interactive way in a relatively short space of time. And because pub quizzes are a form of leisure activity, it should also be fun and enjoyable.

Materials

Pub Quiz on Happiness. Each group will need a single sheet of A4 paper and a pen. A prize for the winning team (optional)

Process/procedure

Format : Seat participants in groups. Announce the structure of the game and 'rules' :
Structure: There will be two parts to the quiz, each with three rounds. Each round will comprise six questions as follows:
- Round 1 is about happiness, health and well-being
- Round 2 is about the sources and causes of happiness
- Round 3 is about who is happiest?
- Round 4 is about your happy chemicals
- Round 5 is about happiness quotations
- Round 6 is about general knowledge about happiness.

'Rules' : There are 2 rules (1) No cheating, and (2) The judge's decision is final even when it is clearly absurd.
Part 1 : Person one reads the questions and Person two keeps score. At end of part 1, person two marks the answers and reads the score so far.
Part 2: As for part 1

End of quiz and prize giving (optional)

Plenary/debrief

None required.

Notes including comments and variations

This quiz is a bit more serious than most pub quizzes – this is because its context is a workshop rather than simply an evening's entertainment in a pub.

Part of the fun of a quiz in a pub is the banter between participants so pub quizzes are usually taken at a leisurely pace. In a happiness workshop the main functions of a pub quiz are to convey knowledge and serve as an ice-breaker. For this reason, it best to facilitate it at a brisk pace.

Pub Quiz

Round 1: Happiness, health and well-being

(The questions in this round are quite serious – so we've made them quite easy)

1. Q "The richest countries in the world have more than doubled their national income over the last 50 years but are no happier." True or False?

A. True

2. Q. Happiness is contagious. By how much does the happiness of a close contact increase our chance of being happy?
a) 5%
b) 10%
c) 15%

A. The answer is about c (15%)

3. Q. "Being happy makes us less at risk of heart attacks" True or false?

A. True

4. Q. "Being happy makes us less likely catch infectious diseases." True or false?

A. True.

5. Q. "Happy people are better at solving problems than unhappy people." True or False?

A. True.

6. Q. Research has shown that people live longer when they have a positive attitude than a negative one. How many years longer, on average?

A. 8 years. We'll accept answers from 6 years to 10 years

Round 2: Sources of happiness

1. Q. Which of the following is associated with lower happiness in the population as a whole?
a) Watching TV
b) Gardening
c) Dancing

A. The answer is a. According to the World Happiness Report: "Many studies have shown that watching TV is associated with lower happiness, other things being equal." (p. 73)

2. Q. People generally become happier as they move from middle age into old age." True or false?

A. True

3. Q. "Studies of Olympic athletes have found that winners of bronze medals are, on average, happier than winners of silver medals." True or false?

A. True. It seems that silver medal winners tend to compare themselves with gold medal winners whereas bronze medal winners tend to compare themselves with those who failed to win any medal.

4. Q. A study of 900 women in paid employment in Texas was carried out in which they were asked to record their activities over the previous day and record how happy each made them? Which of the following activities made them happiest?
a) Talking on the phone
b) Having sex
c) Shopping

A. The answer is b. (Having sex - which scored 4.7 out of a possible 5, then shopping at 3.2, then talking on the phone at 3.1)

5. Q. In 2006, Harvard psychologist, Dan Gilbert, published a book on why humans are so bad at predicting what will make us happy. The first two words of the title is 'Stumbling on". What is the third and final word?

A. 'Happiness'

6. Q. "Money spent on experiences (like holidays) produces more happiness than the same money spent on goods (like new cars)." True or false?

A. True

Round 3: Who is happiest?

1. Q. Which is the happiest country in the world?
a) Thailand
b) Denmark
c) Jamaica

A. Denmark (but it does depend on which survey you are looking at, and which happiness measures are being used. Often Denmark comes near the top, certainly higher than Thailand or Jamaica)

2. Q. A recent study in the UK looked at how happy people are in different careers. In which of the following careers are people happiest, on average:
a) Finance/banking
b) HR/Personnel
c) Gardening/Floristry

A. The answer is c) (Gardening/Floristry). Finance/banking came lowest in terms of happiness

3. Q. Which country officially prioritised Gross National Happiness above Gross National Income as early as 1972?

A. Bhutan

4. Q. "Doing good makes us feel good." True or false?

A. True.

5. Q. "In most developed countries, men are happier than women, on average." True or False?

A. False

6. Q. "On average, people who meditate regularly are happier than people who do not." True or False?

A. True

Part 2: Rounds 4 - 6

Round 4: Your Happy Chemicals

1. Q. There is a chemical known as the 'cuddle hormone' because it makes us feel warmer, more trusting and kinder towards others. What is its name?
a) Insulin
b) Oestrogen
c) Oxytocin

A. The answer is c) (Oxytocin).

2. Q. Which of the following chemicals are released in your brain to give you a lift when you are pursuing and achieving your goals?
a) Trypsin
b) Dopamine
c) Progesterone

A. The answer is b) (Dopamine).

3. Q. Which of the following chemicals is associated with the pursuit of happiness as a result of increased status and respect from other people?
a) Fibrinogen
b) Serotonin
c) Lipase

A. The answer is b) (Serotonin).

4. Q. Which of our neurochemicals helps to mask pain? It is also commonly linked to the so-called 'runners high':
a) Endorphins
b) Rennin
c) Amylase

A. The answer is a) (Endorphins).

5. Q. Physical exercise can increase happiness by reducing levels of a hormone which is associated with stress. Is it:
a) Testosterone
b) Cortisol
c) Prolactin

A. The answer is b). (Cortisol) (Source: Breuning, L. 2012, Ch. 6)

6. Q. Paul Zac is well-known as "Dr Love" as a result of his research on the effects of which of our happy chemicals?

A. Oxytocin

Round 5: Quotes

This round is made up of quotes by the following people, (you may wish to make a note of them):
- William James (founder of modern psychology)
- The Dalai Lama
- Abraham Lincoln
- Benjamin Disraeli
- Buddha
- Aristotle

1. Q. Who said: "Happiness is the meaning and the purpose of life, the whole aim and end of human existence." ?

A. Aristotle

2. Q. Who said "People are just as happy as they make up their minds to be."?

A. Abraham Lincoln.

3. Q. Who said: "Thousands of candles can be lit from a single candle, and the life of the candle will not be shortened. Happiness never decreases by being shared."?

A. Buddha

4. Q. Who said: "Action may not always bring happiness: but there is no happiness without action."?

A. Benjamin Disraeli

5. Q. Who said: "Happiness is not something ready made. It comes from your own actions."?

A. The Dalai Lama

6. Q. Who said: "I don't sing because I'm happy; I'm happy because I sing."?

A. William James

Round 6: Other and miscellaneous general knowledge about happiness

1. Q. "More choice always means more happiness." True or false?

A. False

2. Q. Which song has been sung most in the UK over the last 10 years?

A. 'Happy Birthday'

3. Q. Which bird is the international symbol of happiness?

A. Bluebird

4. Q. According to Charles Schultz, the creator of the Peanuts Cartoons and its hero Charlie Brown, happiness is a warm what?

A. Puppy

5. Q. According to the Beatles, happiness is a warm what?

A. Gun. 'Happiness is a warm gun' (This was featured on the Beatles' White Album)

6. Q. Who sang the hit song 'Don't Worry, Be Happy?'

A. Bobby McFerrin.

Tie-breaker question:

Q. What is the name of the band which had a hit with the song 'Happy Together' which contained the line: 'I can't see me loving nobody but you, for all my life' (sing that line to give the participants the tune)

A. The Turtles.

And if that doesn't separate the winners then the second tie-breaker is:

Q. How many 5-letter words can you make out of the word 'PLEASURE' in the next 4 minutes?

A. Depends on how good each group is with words: e.g. Here are 12 such words: ALURE, SPEAR, SPARE, ERASE, RUPEE, LEAPS, LEERS, PEERS, REAPS, REELS, PLEAS, PEELS

Activity 45
Best Possible Past Life

Action for Happiness Key
Resilience

Individual, pairs

Rationale

According to research by Dan McAdams we can increase our happiness by interpreting our past life in the most positive way possible. It seems to be important for us to be able to make sense of what has happened to us and integrate past experiences in a coherent way. For example, if we can explain past difficulties and misfortunes as necessary experiences to enable us to become the people we are today, then that helps to resolve those difficulties and misfortunes.

Materials

None required.

Process/procedure

1. It seems to be part of being human that we seek meaning in what happens to us. The most usual way of doing this is through stories. A common story is the victim story – we are the victim of something bigger or stronger than us or we are victims of fate or bad luck i.e. victims of what we can't control. The upside of this story is that we avoid responsibility for any of the bad things that happen to us and we don't beat ourselves up. The downside is that we give up our power and convince ourselves that we are weaker than we actually are and have less control over our world. And, generally, happiness is associated with a belief that we have control over our world and our life.

2. People who suffer a trauma which they can't make much sense of are likely to suffer post-traumatic stress whereas people who can interpret the trauma in a positive way or find meaning in it are more likely to experience post-traumatic growth.

3. One alternative to the victim's story is the hero/heroine's journey. In this case the hero/heroine overcomes obstacles and misfortune to win through in the end. The ultimate goal of the hero is invariably something bigger and more inspiring than the self. The story inspires us to doing the right thing, serving a larger goal and eventually triumphing over that which oppressed us, misfortune, or things that got in the way.

4. Find a partner and tell your own story as a story of triumph over the obstacles, pitfalls and misfortunes that have got in the way but have enabled you to become the person you are today. If possible tell how the obstacles and misfortunes played a part in developing the good parts of your character. Remember Nietzsche's words 'That which does not kill me makes me stronger'. (10 minutes each way)

Plenary/debrief

Ask who found they had something or some things in common with their partner.
How can you reframe the worst things that have happened to you as stepping stones to the person you've become?
Would it help to write your 'hero's story' in your happiness journal?

Activity 46
Blissful Guided Imagery

Action for Happiness Key
Emotion

Individual

Rationale

This simple visualisation exercise demonstrates the power of the mind to alter our moods and to create a more happy mental state. It should also be a relaxing and ultimately enjoyable experience for all participants.

Materials

The guided imagery script (see below). This script is available as a free resource from www.the-guided-meditation-site.com/blissful-mind-guided-meditation-script.html

Process/procedure

This script uses plenty of guided imagery to lead you into a state of deep relaxation, and then opens your heart and mind to experience a natural state of bliss. It is a peaceful and positive guided meditation that lasts for about 15 - 20 minutes.

Plenary/debrief

Ask participants to share their experience of the activity in pairs.

- What did you notice?
- What made the activity difficult?
- What made it easy to do?
- How might you continue to do more (guided or unguided) visualisation exercises at home?

Notes including comments and variations

You might ask participants to spend a few moments describing in their happiness journals how they feel before the activity and then to do the same afterwards. What differences do they notice?

Blissful Visualisation Script

Welcome to this guided meditation.
Please find yourself a quiet place to sit and dim the lights.
Make sure that you are nice and comfortable. Loosen any tight clothing.
Let your hands rest loosely in your lap. Now close your eyes...and relax.
With your eyes closed, you begin to connect with your inner world of thought and feeling.
Gradually, the external world will fade from your awareness.
For the next few minutes, give yourself permission to enjoy this relaxing experience.
You are free from all your responsibilities at this time, so put aside any thoughts of tasks or concerns that may be waiting for you.
If you find that your mind wanders during this meditation, simply bring your awareness back to the sound of my voice, and I will guide you to a place of deep relaxation and inner stillness.
Remember that you are always in control. If you wish to stop at any time, you can do so by simply opening your eyes.
Now take a long, slow, deep breath in...and then release that breath.
Feel yourself relaxing.
Again, take a long, slow, deep breath in...and then let that breath go.
Take another deep breath in...and exhale completely.
Notice how calming it is to breathe this way. Notice the feelings of relaxation that are beginning to spread throughout your whole body.
Continue to breathe slowly, deeply and gently.
With each breath you take, your thoughts become lighter.
You may sense a feeling of spaciousness opening up inside you.
Relax now.
Allow the gentle movement of your breath to guide you into an even more relaxed state.
In... and out... and deeper you go.
In... and out... allow your mind to gradually slow down all by itself.
In... and out...
You are now in a state of relaxation, and it's time to enjoy a guided journey to an inner place of serenity and bliss.
As I speak, just allow images to form in your mind naturally, in your own time.
If mental pictures don't come easily to you, then simply sense your imagined surroundings rather than seeing them.
Let go of all your expectations, and allow yourself to experience this guided journey in whatever way comes naturally to you.
Imagine that you are standing in a beautiful grassy field.
You can feel the warmth of the sun on your face and body.
You can feel the lush green grass, soft beneath your bare feet.
You can hear the sounds of nature around you.
You are very much at home in this peaceful place.
You have all the time in the world.
You feel safe and happy here.
Take a moment to appreciate your surroundings...
You notice a large tree growing nearby.
Begin to walk towards the tree.
Take your time. Be in the moment and experience each step.
As you walk, feel yourself slipping even more deeply into a state of total relaxation.
Now you stand beneath the tree. Its strong branches and broad leaves hang right over your head.
Notice that the tree is covered in delicious fruits of many shapes, sizes and colours.
This is no ordinary tree. Its fruits contain special powers.

Reach up and take a piece of fruit from the tree. Study it for a moment. Notice the colour, the texture, the weight of it in your hand.

Now take a bite.

As the fruit slides down your throat and into your stomach, something wonderful begins to happen…

A feeling of happiness begins to glow deep inside you.

The sensation begins in your stomach, and then it spreads to your chest and your heart.

Let go of thinking, and concentrate on feeling. Nurture this sensation of happiness and love. Feel yourself gently glowing with it.

Take another bite of the fruit now. Taste it. Savour it.

Now the wonderful feeling intensifies a little more.

Feel yourself gently radiating this pleasant sensation of love and happiness.

Now take a third bite of the fruit, take as much as you want.

Relax and allow yourself to swell up with this delightful feeling. Don't try. Just let it rise effortlessly within you. Allow it to increase as much as you like.

Stay with these blissful feelings and enjoy this time of peaceful meditation.

You can remain in this relaxed state of meditation for as long as you like.

If you would like to finish this meditation, you may do so at any time. When you are ready, simply open your eyes. Please give yourself a few minutes to adjust before you get up.

This script is available as a free resource from www.the-guided-meditation-site.com/blissful-mind-guided-meditation-script.html

Activity 47
Integrated Meditation

Action for Happiness Key
Emotion

Individual

Rationale
Research suggests that practising meditation contributes to greater happiness and well-being, as well as lower stress, anxiety and depression. This simple activity will allow participants to experience four different types of meditation in a very short space of time. They may find that one type of meditation is more effective for them than another, or that they like the variety of 4-in-1.

Materials
None required.

Process/procedure
1. Explain the purpose of the activity.
2. Ask the participants to find a comfortable position, sitting (on a chair or on the floor) or standing.
3. Spend 1 minute concentrating on your breathing. Notice the rise and fall of your chest as you breathe in and as you breathe out. If you catch yourself thinking about something else just gently take your awareness back to your breathing.
4. For 1 minute extend your awareness to your whole body – notice how your whole body feels as you breathe in and breathe out.
5. Spend 1 minute becoming aware of the physical sensations in your body, your feelings and thoughts.

6. For 1 minute, think of someone you care about and silently intone the mantra:
   May you be safe / May you be healthy and strong / May you be happy /May you be peaceful and at peace

7. Next spend 1 minute silently intoning the mantra:
   May I be safe / May I be healthy and strong / May I be happy / May I be peaceful and at peace

8. Finally, spend 1 minute silently intoning the mantra:
   May all beings be safe / May all beings be healthy and strong / May all beings be happy / May all beings be peaceful and at peace

Plenary/debrief
- What did you find most difficult in that? What did you enjoy most? How do you feel now?

Notes including comments and variations
You could increase the time for each parts of the process (e.g. 1 minute for the first part, 2 minutes for the second, 3 for the third etc.

Activity 48
Connections and Friendship

Action for Happiness Key
Relating, Trying Out

Individual, pairs

Rationale

One of the most frequently quoted findings from positive psychology is that relationships are one of the most important contributors to our happiness. One feature that distinguishes very happy people is not their money, status or material possessions but the fact that they have a good social life, they have friends and a romantic partner. The value of our connections and friendships is not to be underestimated.

Materials

Handout: Ingredients of Friendship Scale.

Process/procedure

1. Introduce this activity in terms of the rationale above and with some remarks about friendship being a skill. Say that some people have a natural talent for friendship whereas for others it takes practice.
2. Ask the participants to rate themselves on the 'Ingredients of Friendship' scale.
3. Ask participants to note down three actions they can take to strengthen their friendship with some person in their lives.
4. Discuss with a partner which actions they are going to take and why.

Plenary/debrief

- Which aspects of friendship are you strong on?
- What actions will you take to strengthen their friendship?

Notes including comments and variations

If you don't want to use the Ingredients of Friendship Scale, here is a contrasting perspective:

1. To lay the groundwork for a friendship show an interest in the other person. You could for example, ask some non-intrusive questions or offer them encouragement in whatever they are doing.

2. As a friendship starts to develop make it clear that you are willing to invest time in the relationship. A good way to do this is to establish some ritual that enables you to spend time together on a regular basis. Examples include regular emails or texts, a weekly visit to the gym, regular meetings for coffee and a catch-up, joint holidays together, a monthly lunch together, etc.

3. Be prepared to reveal your personal thoughts and feelings. Self-disclosure by you encourages self-disclosure by your new friend and that develops intimacy, which deepens a friendship.

4. Listen attentively to your friend's issues and disclosures. It is not enough to be interested, you also need to *convey* your interest to your friend. Make eye-contact and acknowledge what you hear, possibly

by reflecting back the gist of it to your friend.

5. When your friend is recounting a problem, describing a difficult situation or revealing some personal thoughts or feelings, avoid switching the attention back to yourself. Avoid responding with words like "That reminds of a time when I ..." or "I know exactly how you feel..." And don't try to 'top' your friend's account with a more extreme story about yourself.

6. Avoid giving uninvited advice and certainly don't press advice. A friend will normally tell you when they want your advice. Often the advice of others can seem like an added burden especially if it necessitates convincing the advice-giver why their advice really won't work in the case in question.

7. Be supportive. One of the great values of friendship is mutual support. A person is stronger and safer with a group of friends than alone. Supporting others when they need it increases the likelihood that they will support you when you need it.

8. Celebrate your friends' successes. Enjoy basking in their reflected glory rather than becoming envious.

9. Defend your friends when they are absent. Stand up for your friends and if possible stand up for the friends of your friends.

10. Hug your friends. Hugging strengthens friendship and intimacy. As a broad generalisation men seem to find it more difficult to hug other men than women to hug other women. Perhaps the best advice is just to hug a few more people than you do now and hug a bit more often.

Handout: Ingredients of Friendship Scale

Give yourself a score from 1 to 5 (where 1 means 'not at all like you' and 5 means 'very much like you') for each of the following aspects of friendship:

- Volunteers help in time of need
- Respects the privacy of the other.
- Keeps confidences
- Trusts and confides in one another
- Stands up for the other in public
- Don't criticise each other in public
- Shows emotional support
- Looks him/her in the eye during conversation
- Strives to make him/her happy while in each other's company
- Not be jealous or critical of each other's relationships
- Tolerant of each other's friends
- Shares news of success with each other
- Asks for personal advice
- Doesn't nag
- Engages in joking or teasing with the friend
- Seeks to repay debts, favours and compliments
- Discloses personal feelings or problems to the friend.

The maximum score is 85, the minimum is 17.

The Friendship Scale comes from The Rules of Friendship by M. Argyle and M. Henderson (1984).

Activity 49
One Small Piece of Chocolate

Action for Happiness Key
Emotion, Relating

Pairs

Rationale

Studies have found that eating dark chocolate can trigger the release of 'happy chemicals' dopamine, endorphins and serotonin. Similarly, feeding others can release the 'happy chemical' oxytocin. This activity is an opportunity not only to do something for someone else, but also to express appreciation to others for what they do for you. It also gives participants a chance to try something that might be new to them.

Materials

Small piece of chocolate per person (and small pieces of dried mango for people who can't eat chocolate).

Process/procedure

1. Ask participants to find a partner, preferably someone they don't know.

2. Each pair gets two small pieces of good quality dark chocolate (or dried mango).

3. The rule of this game is that no-one can eat chocolate they pick up themselves. So one of the partners offers a piece of chocolate to the other partner ... who presumably accepts with a 'thank you'.

4. Partner one then feeds a piece of the chocolate to partner two who savours the experience of eating it for 1 minute.

5. Partner two then feeds the other piece of chocolate to partner one who savours the experience of eating it for 1 minute. And then thanks partner two.

Plenary/debrief

- Briefly review what happened in this activity and ask the participants for any observations or comments on the experience.
- What were you thinking as you did that activity? What feelings did you experience?
- Can you see any connections with that experience and the Action for Happiness keys to happiness:
    - Giving
    - Relationship
    - Appreciation
    - Trying out new things?

Notes including comments and variations

Have some water available for anyone who fears for their teeth.

You could 'gift-wrap' the chocolates as tiny presents.

Activity 50
Vocational Mapping

Action for Happiness Key
Trying Out, Direction

Individual

Rationale

The good life is not one of victory and triumphs but one of a satisfying and intrinsically motivated daily life. As Bob Dylan said, " A man is a success if he gets up in the morning and goes to bed at night and in between does what he wants to do."

The purpose of this exercise is to shift the focus from salary- and career-oriented thinking towards thinking about the enjoyment of an activity itself. It can also enable participants to discover the activities which they find intrinsically motivating and could even help them to discover a vocation.

Materials

Pen and paper, happiness journal or smart phone for note-taking. A supporting list of activities which you need to prepare in advance

Process/procedure

1. Introduce the activity: the goal of this task is to map out what is intrinsically motivating and vocational to you. The idea is to write down everything you enjoy doing for its own sake, not because of an external reward or threat. We will also look at how your intrinsically motivated activities might contribute to your calling (vocation).

2. Hand out the sheets of paper.

3. Ask the participants to list all the things they enjoy doing simply for the sake of doing them. Include work activities, hobbies and even dreams. Do not include basic physiological needs such as eating, sleeping and sex. Focus on such activities that elicit the 'flow' experience in people. Give a few examples, such as 'reading', 'riding a horse', 'drawing', 'gardening', 'boating' etc.

4. If you want you can hand out or project on a screen a supporting list of activities (at least two dozen different examples) that the participants can consult if they can't think of anything new. Have the list ready on a handout, flip chart or a slide if you're using Power Point.

5. Ask the participants to score each activity according to how often they get to practise it in their current life situation.
- Score 3 for each activity that the participant gets to do just as much as they want already in their lives. In other words, they're not lacking in time, money or other resource to pursue this activity.
- Score 2 for each activity that the participant gets to do a great deal but would gladly do more if he/she had more resources such as time or money.
- Score 1 for each activity that the participant can only do rarely or not at all.

Allow participants one minute to complete this.

6. Inform the participants that they now have a map of two things: their vocational life, in which the majority of waking hours would be made up of the activities on the map; i.e. where practically every item on the list would get a score of three. And their present situation; how far removed are they from their vocational life?

7. In order to apply the information in practice, ask the participants to consult the list and think up variations of what kinds of jobs or professions they could pursue so that the needed resources (time, money etc) would be produced by the activities on the list. Emphasise that it does not matter which activities produce the livelihood and which are hobbies.

8. Give a few examples; for example, a person enjoying driving, performing and reading could be at teacher (performing and reading as livelihood with driving as a hobby) or a truck driver (driving as a livelihood, performing and reading as a hobby).

Plenary/debrief

Discuss briefly and discreetly the options that the participants discovered using the activity. Emphasise that it may take some time and self-reflection to discover applicable strategies.

Activity 51
Signature Strengths

Action for Happiness Key
Trying Out, Direction

Individual, pairs

Rationale

One of the most compelling pieces of positive psychology research concerns using strengths in new ways. It has been found that people who use their strengths in new ways every day for a week experienced an uplift in happiness and well-being and a reduction in symptoms of depression for up to 6 months later.

Materials

A copy of the VIA4 questionnaire for each participant from pages 243-265 of Martin Seligman's book 'Flourish' or downloaded from:
www.authentichappiness.org or from www.viastrengths.org.

One copy of the handout on '340 ways to use VIA character strengths by Rashid and Anjum (2005). This is available at:
www.actionforhappiness.org/media/52486/340_ways_to_use_character_strengths.pdf

Process/procedure

1. Introduce the activity in terms of the reasons for doing it (see above).

2. Invite participants to identify their signature strengths by completing the VIA strengths questionnaire.

3. Take one of the signature strengths you've identified and work out where and how you can use that strength in a new way three times in the next week. You can probably think of new ways on your own but we also have a handout with some suggestions produced by Tayyab Rashid and Afroze Anjum (2005) which you might find helpful.

4. Find a partner and compare what you have come up with. Arrange to phone or email each other after a week to compare the impact of doing this on your happiness.

Plenary/debrief

- Share some of the signature strengths you've found and how you are going to use them.
- Did your top strengths resonate with you? i.e. do you agree that they are your top strengths? Why?
- Let this lead into a discussion about living a more strengths-based life.

Activity 52
Giving Positive Feedback on Strengths

Action for Happiness Key
Giving, Relating, Emotion

Individual

Rationale

One of our aims in writing this book is to encourage participants to take actions that will raise the likelihood of their living happier lives. Some of these actions will increase their own happiness directly, and some will do so indirectly. This activity goes further, in that we are asking participants to help the people they care about to live lives that are more effective and happier. This activity enables people we care about to discover personal strengths and positive qualities that they may not be aware of, and in doing so we are promoting feelings of happiness and well-being beyond ourselves.

Materials

Handout: Giving Positive Feedback on Strengths.

Process/procedure

1. Introduce the reasons for doing this exercise and explain that the aim is to produce a draft letter to someone you care about providing them with feedback on three or four strengths or positive qualities.

2. Think of a person who you care about, probably a family member or a friend. Then spend a few minutes thinking about what you like about that person and perhaps some good times you've shared together and times you've been impressed by them. Then make a mind-map of what you see as their positive qualities, talents and personal strengths.

3. List two or three things about this person that you (1) admire, (2) value, (3) respect and (4) appreciate.

4. You now have the raw material to write a letter to this person identifying what you see as their strengths, talents and positive qualities.

5. Read through the 'Letter to Jane' handout which you can use as a template. Note that when you list the three or four strengths, talents and positive qualities they will appreciate having specific examples. Using examples will make your letter more grounded and less abstract.

Plenary/debrief

- Ask participants who they wrote their letter to.
- Ask them to commit to writing up their draft as a final version, even if they never send it. Ask them to get to the point where it is in an envelope and all they have to do is post it.
- Ask them what they think the response would be if they actually did send the letter.

Notes including comments and variations

You could consider sending a 'Strengths letter' to someone as a birthday present.

Handout: Giving Positive Feedback on Strengths

Letter to Jane

Dear Jane

Some months ago my daughter Sally asked me how school education in Britain could be improved. I said I'd like to see schools focus much more on identifying talents and strengths (non-academic as well as academic). My reason was if school-leavers had a good understanding of their talents and strengths they would be in a much better position to live richer, more fulfilling, lives and to achieve their goals in life.

Afterwards I thought that if school doesn't do this then family and friends are also in a position to do so. So I wrote Sally a letter to give her some feedback on her talents/strengths that I've recognised in recent years, which she really appreciated. As one of your oldest friends I think I'm in a position to recognise some of your talents too. So here, and in no particular order, are some that I've noticed:

Good sense of humour (and infectious laugh): this makes you an enjoyable work colleague and good company when not working.

Ability to mix easily with people from different social backgrounds: I seem to remember you had friends from all strata of society when you were at Birmingham and you seem to be able to mix with City folk as well as you mix with East End folk.

Articulate: You seem to be able to express your thoughts very clearly and often with wit and a dry sense of humour.

Dependable, 'steady as a rock': This is a talent/strength you have brought to every project you've taken on since I've known you.

Pro-active: I've been impressed by your initiative and your 'give it a go' attitude. It seems to me you are inclined to ask 'why not?' rather than 'why?'.

I'm reluctant to go on in case you think that what I neglect to mention indicates a deficit.

With love and best wishes

Tom

Activity 53
Questions for Happiness

Action for Happiness Key
Emotion

Individual, pairs

Rationale

The purpose of most of the activities in this book is to enhance participants' positive feelings so that they leave the workshop feeling happier than when they arrived. Science shows us that how we think and how we feel are closely connected. So if we can change how we think, for example think more positively, we can also change how we feel, and feel happier.

This exercise is also aimed at enhancing participants' positive feelings, but it does so by asking questions which evoke positive thoughts, that is, thoughts about people, places and experiences which have positive associations for us. Finally, it gives participants the opportunity to capitalise on these positive feelings by sharing the experience with others in the group.

Materials

Happiness journal and handout: Happy Thoughts Questionnaire.

Process/procedure

1. Give everyone the list of 20 questions which are intended to elicit happy thoughts and ask them to write their answers in their happiness journals.

2. Ask each person to find a partner, preferably someone they don't already know, and share the three happiest thoughts generated by the questions.

Plenary/debrief

- Who found it easy to answer the questions? Who found it difficult?
- Which questions were easiest? And which were most difficult?
- Who had a particularly happy thought they are willing to share?

Handout: Happy Thoughts Questionnaire

1. What place in your life has happy associations?

2. What person in your life has happy associations?

3. Give the title of one song or piece of music that makes you happy. Can you think of something that makes your heart sing?

4. What was your happiest holiday?

5. What was your favourite birthday (your own or someone you care about.)

6. Give the name of one person you love.

7. What is the name of one person who loves you or who has loved you?

8. List two things you are good at.

9. List two times you have felt fulfilled.

10. List two things you've done that you feel proud about.

11. Recall a time when you've been happy on your own.

12. Recall a time when you've been happy with other people.

13. What is one thing which gives meaning or a sense of purpose to your work/life?

14. List two things that you are looking forward to this year

15. List three good things that happened to you this week.

16. What one piece of good news can you share with others today?

17. What is your happiest memory?

18. Name two people you have smiled at today

19. Which two people have smiled at you today?

20. List three things that you really appreciate about where you live.

Activity 54
Quotes about Happiness

Action for Happiness Key
Trying Out

Individual, pairs

Rationale

Popular quotes are popular because they convey meaning that resonates with many people. This exercise introduces some popular quotes about happiness and introduces the participants to the some of the leading thinkers on the subject. It also gives them the opportunity to explore more deeply what happiness means to them, and to hear alternative perspectives and ideas which are often very enlightening.

Materials

Handout: Quotes about Happiness.

Process/procedure

1. Introduce the activity as an opportunity to consider what leading thinkers have had to say about happiness.

2. Ask participants to each identify the three quotes that resonate most strongly with them – or at least the ones they find most thought-provoking.

3. Ask each person to find a partner, preferably someone they don't already know, and explain why they chose the three quotes that they did.

Plenary/debrief

Which three quotes did each person choose? Do a tally to find the most popular quote(s).

Ask the participants what it is about that quote that made them choose it.

Do the same with the next most popular quote. And possibly also the next one, depending on the time you have for this activity.

Handout: Quotes about Happiness

"Happiness is the meaning and the purpose of life, the whole aim and end of human existence." - **Aristotle**

"People are just as happy as they make up their minds to be." - **Abraham Lincoln**

"Thousands of candles can be lit from a single candle, and the life of the candle will not be shortened. Happiness never decreases by being shared." - **The Buddha**

"Action may not always bring happiness: but there is no happiness without action." - **Benjamin Disraeli**

"Happiness is not something ready made. It comes from your own actions." - **Dalai Lama**

"I don't sing because I'm happy; I'm happy because I sing." - **William James**

"The purpose of our lives is to be happy." - **Dalai Lama**

"Whoever is happy will make others happy." - **Anne Frank**

"It is the greatest happiness of the greatest number that is the measure of right and wrong." – **Jeremy Bentham**

"Success is not the key to happiness. Happiness is the key to success." – **Albert Schweitzer**

Activity 55
Inner Sage

Action for Happiness Key
Trying Out, Direction, Meaning

Individual

Rationale

Sometimes we are more willing to take advice from ourselves than from other people. The purpose of this exercise is to capture some of the lessons we've personally learned about living a happier life and to reinforce them in the form of a letter to the self.

Materials

Happiness journals and handout: Inner Sage.

Process/procedure

1. Introduce the activity in terms of the rationale for the activity as above.

2. Imagine you are half as old as you are now - think back to that time. Take 5 minutes to give yourself advice to your younger self on how to find more happiness in your life. Make notes in your happiness journal. Be as specific as you can. For example, if your older, wiser self advises you to spend more time with your family then you might want to be specific about how you might do this e.g. an additional weekly family outing.

3. Now imagine that you are 20 years older than you now are. Take 5 minutes to give yourself advice on how to find more happiness in your life starting from where you are now. Do this activity in writing – making notes in your happiness journal. Be as specific as you can.

4. Distribute the handout or read the examples aloud

Plenary/debrief

What sorts of advice did participants give to their younger selves to increase their happiness?
What sorts of advice did their older, wiser selves give to their present selves to increase their happiness?
What sorts of things are participants likely to do as a result of this exercise?

Notes including comments and variations

There is a regular item in the *Big Issue* titled 'Letter to My Younger Self' whereby people are asked to write a letter to themselves at the age of 16 about the things that were worrying them then and offering them advice. You could use this format instead of the one above. Or you could just ask participants what the person they are now would like to say to their 16-year old selves.

Handout: Inner Sage: Example 1

Dear Emma-Jayne (aged 22)

Try not to fret too much about getting the 'right' job. Lots of people have several different careers in their lifetime because they develop new skills and interests as they get older and meet new people, and remember that new opportunities will always come along if you remain open to them. Find ways to play to your strengths at work, developing other people and look for ways to build new relationships inside and outside of work, because this is where the opportunities will appear. Make sure your values are in line with those of the organisation you want to work for – it will save a lot of soul-searching, and you'll be far happier at work as well as at home.

Remember also to spend time with Nana, she's a great source of inspiration and comfort when you're feeling down.

Love from Emma-Jayne (aged 44)

Handout: Inner Sage: Example 2

Dear Emma-Jayne (aged 44)

You're doing a great job of balancing work and home life at the moment. One thing I can think of that would make a difference is to be more mindful when you are at home and with the family. Keep practising mindfulness techniques and develop a greater focus on the present. Even just a few minutes a day will help you feel calmer and less stressed. The kids really do value the time you spend with them so give it a go.
I know you're not a great fan of setting goals, so why not try visualisation instead? Imagine how you'd feel being healthier, and fitter. The kids would be very proud of you too, and you might win the parents' race at sports day next year!

Love from Emma-Jayne (aged 64)

Activity 56
Finding Happiness Outside the Comfort Zone

Action for Happiness Key
Trying Out

Individual

Rationale

This is a very useful exercise for demonstrating experientially how difficult it is to change behaviour, and how any change (even positive change such as greater happiness) requires effort, determination and constant practice. It also prepares participants for action planning for greater happiness.

Materials

None required.

Process/procedure

1. Ask participants to fold their arms.

2. Do a tally of the number of participants
   - With their right arm on top of their left arm
   - With their left arm on top of their right arm.

3. Ask participants to refold their arms the 'opposite' way.

4. Ask for feedback about how the new way feels. People will respond with statements like "I had to think carefully to fold my arms the 'other' way" and "It feels uncomfortable".

Plenary/debrief

Relate this experience to the challenge of living a happier life. Point out that nearly all change feels uncomfortable – that applies to both attitudinal change and behavioural change. Changing our lives to make them happier is likely to involve stepping out of our comfort zones. So we need to be patient with ourselves and exercise self-compassion. Encourage participants to set realistic goals and expectations about their behaviour following the workshop.

Another point: changing our lives to make them happier is likely to require conscious thought in areas where we've been on automatic pilot.

You can press home the point by asking participants who are wearing a watch to switch it to the other wrist. Ask them to comment on how that feels. Then ask them to leave their watches on the 'wrong' wrist for the rest of the workshop (or over lunch) as a reminder that changing to a happier life is likely to involve stepping out of their comfort zones temporarily.

Activity 57
Happiness Quotations

Action for Happiness Key
Emotion, Meaning

Individual

Rationale

This is a good exercise to break the ice, get people in a positive frame of mind and inspire them to find (or create) their own happiness quotation.

It reminds us that despite the recent emergence of positive psychology, people have been interested in happiness since the dawn of time.

Materials

One pre-printed quotation about happiness and well-being (sourced from Google) per pair of participants, cut up as illustrated in these examples:

- *Don't cry/because/it's over,/smile/because/it happened* (**Dr Seuss**)
- *Happiness is/when/what you think,/what you say,/ and/what you do/are in harmony* (***Mahatma Gandhi***)
- *Happiness is/not/something/ready-made./ It comes/from/ your own/actions* (***Dalai Lama***)

Flip charts & blu-tack (optional)

Process/procedure

1. Give each pair a happiness quotation cut into sections to unscramble.

2. You might ask them to write the unscrambled quotation on a flip chart and stick them around the walls.

Plenary/debrief

Ask participants to read and comment on their quotation, and/or their favourite quotation

Activity 58
Tokens of Appreciation

Action for Happiness Key
Giving, Appreciating, Relating

Individual

Rationale

Expressing your gratitude towards people who have helped you has been shown by research to have a long-lasting impact on your well-being. This is a fun, creative exercise in which participants are encouraged to create their own 'token of appreciation' in the form of a beaded bracelet, charm or necklace.

Materials

A wide variety of beads of different colours, sizes and textures. Wire, cord or elastic for threading. Scissors.

A plastic bucket or tray per pair / group

Process/procedure

1. Divide participants into pairs or small groups of 4-6.

2. Give each pair/group a bucket/tray of beads, scissors and enough thread for each participant to create their own token.

3. Instruct each participant to create a bracelet, charm or necklace. For each bead that they add, each participant shares something that they're grateful for with their partner/group.

4. When they have finished they can nominate a person to give the token of appreciation to, and say why they have selected that person.

5. The person receiving the token may be another workshop member or someone else.

Plenary/debrief

Participants can share with the whole group how they felt about expressing their gratitude in this way.

Notes including comments and variations

Participants can make a bracelet to keep instead, as a reminder of all the things they are thankful for.

Activity 59
Strengths Date

Action for Happiness Key
Giving, Emotion, Relating

Individual, pairs

Rationale

Research suggests that applying your strengths in new ways every day is an effective way to boost your well-being and reduce depressive symptoms over the longer term. This activity familiarises participants with the language of the 'Values in Action' (VIA) strengths inventory (www.authentichappiness.org or www.viame.org) and has them focus on putting their top strengths into practice. The objective is for each participant to plan a 'Strengths Date' for themselves and a partner which they put into practice.

Materials

None, but participants must complete the VIA-IS inventory (either 120 or 240 question versions, but not the 'brief' version) in advance and be aware of their Top 5 strengths.

Process/procedure

1. Participants imagine that they have a whole day to enjoy with a spouse, partner or close friend, in which to indulge their respective strengths. Ask them to imagine what activities they would do to play to their strengths.

2. Have them plan a whole day focussing on these activities. What would they choose and why?

3. Give examples if necessary: someone with 'Appreciation of Beauty and Excellence' as a top strength might choose to visit an art gallery, or watch a sunset from a local viewpoint. Someone with the strength of humour might go to a comedy club or put on a comedy night at their local pub. Someone with the strength of curiosity might go to a restaurant featuring a cuisine they have never tried before, and so on.

4. It may be beneficial to work in pairs, brainstorming ideas.

Plenary/debrief

Ask participants to share their Strengths Date plans with the group.

Notes including comments and variations

Ask participants to organise and carry out their Strengths Date with their partner as planned and to report back at a later session.

Activity 60
Good News Stories

Action for Happiness Key
Emotion, Appreciating

Small groups

Rationale

Evolutionary psychologists have suggested that we have an inbuilt 'negativity bias', that we have evolved to notice negative things before we notice positive ones. As a result, we need to acquire an appreciative bias by 'retraining' our brains to notice all the positive things around us. This activity enables participants to start honing their 'appreciative eye'.

Materials

One newspaper per team – you can use free papers like the London Evening Standard or Metro, or a selection of daily papers.

Process/procedure

1. Give each group a copy of a newspaper.

2. Have them look for as many positive, uplifting news stories as they can.

3. Ask each group to select their favourite positive story to share with the group, what they liked about it and how it made them feel.

Plenary/debrief

Ask participants to suspend judgement when listening to feedback; what other people find uplifting may not work for everyone. Comments such as 'I didn't like that story because....' tend to dampen the mood.

Notes including comments and variations

You can ask participants to look for stories on a specific theme or strength, such as demonstrations of courage, fairness, trust and so on.

Ask participants to experiment with monitoring their daily intake of media (radio, TV, newspapers, online, celebrity magazines). Can they exercise self-control and limit what they consume? What happens to their mood over time when they purposefully focus on good news stories instead? Take feedback in a subsequent workshop.

Activity 61
Strengths Notes

Action for Happiness Key
Emotion, Relating, Giving, Appreciating

Individual

Rationale

This is a great exercise to use at the end of a workshop, to ensure that everyone leaves feeling upbeat and optimistic. It also reinforces people's understanding and appreciation of their personal strengths, and helps them feel validated and cared for.

Materials

Pens and plenty of Post-it notes.

Process/procedure

1. Ask each participant to think about the strengths that have been displayed by other participants during the course of the workshop. These might be VIA strengths or any other talents and gifts. Try to find at least two strengths/talents/gifts per person.

2. Ask them to write one strength/talent/gift per Post-it, and to stick it to the 'owner's' back.

3. At the end of the activity, each participant can retrieve, read and keep the Post-its that they have been given. Every participant will have a small collection of notes which validate their personal strengths which they can keep in their happiness journals and refer to when they need a boost.

Plenary/debrief

None required.

Activity 62
Secret Notes

Action for Happiness Key
Emotion, Relating, Giving, Appreciating

Individual

Rationale

Making other people in our lives feel loved, appreciated and special to us is an important part of building and sustaining strong relationships. Expressing and sharing our positive emotions (love, gratitude, excitement etc.) also makes us feel good.

This is a great little activity to do for homework, though you can have participants prepare their secret notes now or brainstorm ideas for what they will do later and to share their ideas in the workshop.

Materials

Post-it notes and pens.

Process/procedure

Write a note (or a series of notes, say one for every day of the week) to your child, partner, friend or colleague and leave it where they will find it later (e.g. attached to the car steering wheel, in a lunch box, inside the fridge, on their PC). The note could be a joke, a personal poem, an 'I Love You' note or a note of appreciation for something they've done (remembering to express how it made you feel).

Plenary/debrief

You can ask participants to share their ideas. You can also ask them to anticipate how their loved one might respond, and how they themselves would respond if someone left them a secret note.

Notes including comments and variations

If used as a homework exercise, remember to take feedback in your next session.

Activity 63
Nature's Treasures

Action for Happiness Key
Appreciating, Emotion, Meaning

Individual

Rationale

Spending time outdoors has long been known to be beneficial to our well-being. Even if we are 'outdoors people' by nature, we're often too busy to notice what is going on around us. This activity encourages participants to use their sense of sight, hearing, smell and touch to reconnect with the natural world.

The exercise combines being outside in nature with gratitude and savouring. Both savouring and expressing appreciation or thanks for normal, everyday events and experiences have been shown to be effective ways to increase happiness. Savouring is a straightforward process which requires your active engagement to enjoy the event or experience in front of you by prolonging it and involving all your senses.

Materials

A garden, park or other green outdoor space with plenty of comfortable seating areas or benches. You may like to take cushions or rugs to sit on.

Process/procedure

Let participants know that they will be spending some time outdoors and that their job is merely to notice and to savour every experience they notice. The exercise is best done seated for steps 1-3, and with eyes closed for steps 2-4.

1. Ask participants to find somewhere quiet and comfortable to sit, and use their sense of sight to notice things around them. Perhaps they notice the way the breeze ripples gently through the grass, the way the sunlight dapples the leaves, the clouds drifting across the sky, or the contrail left by a jet way up high.

2. Use the sense of hearing to notice and savour all the different sounds – loud, quiet, soft, harsh, high-pitched and so on (birds, lawnmowers, distant traffic, people whistling, humming, kids playing, insects buzzing etc.).

3. Use the sense of smell – faint, strong, fresh, floral, musty, light, wispy, natural, like chemicals and so on (newly mown grass, cooking smells, traffic, flowers, sun-cream, perfume etc).

4. Use the sense of touch (the warm fur of a pet cat, sand, grass or concrete under bare feet, the feel of the leaves or bark of plants and trees – smooth, hairy, rough, spiky etc.).

5. Once participants have used all four senses, ask them to repeat the exercise, aiming to notice even more the second time around.

Plenary/debrief

Take feedback from participants, asking them to describe some of their experiences. Ensure that they make a connection between the savouring and their heightened well-being. Ask them how they might introduce more savouring into their lives.

Notes including comments and variations

This activity can be done in all weathers (different seasons provide different opportunities) though most people will prefer warm, dry, sunny days. Participants will need season-appropriate clothing, and sunglasses or sun-screen on very hot days.

Discourage participants from simply 'listing' what they see, smell, hear or touch; it's not a competition to see who can notice the most things, it's about the quality of the experience, and about slowing down long enough to reconnect with the natural world.

There are several other savouring and gratitude-based activities listed in the index.

Activity 64
Life through a Lens

Action for Happiness Key
Trying out, Resilience, Acceptance, Meaning

Individual

Rationale

Psychologists suggest that our inbuilt negativity bias i.e. taking more notice of the bad things in our lives than the good things, is a survival mechanism. Making time to reflect on the positive and adaptive experiences in our lives, and to share them with other people, can therefore be a useful reminder of what brings us happiness, and an effective way to build appreciation for the good things we already have in our lives. You might also gain additional insights into your part in making these positive experiences come about, your strengths and talents, the new doors which opened as a result of overcoming difficulties, and the supportive role of other people in your life.

Materials

Pen and paper, happiness journal or smart phone for note-taking.
Somewhere comfortable and quiet to sit and reflect – this could be indoors or outside

Process/procedure

1. Explain that taking time to review your life from a positive perspective is time well spent. Not only does this help sharpen your appreciative bias and diminish your negativity bias, it helps you develop a stronger sense of yourself, your strengths and talents and the supportive relationships in your life.

2. Have participants consider the following six questions:
    - What achievements am I most proud of in my life?
    - What is the most important lesson that I've learned from my life that is worth sharing with others?
    - How did I overcome the difficulties in my life?
    - What are the most meaningful moments in my life?
    - What are the happiest moments in my life?
    - Who has been the most kind and helpful to me and for whom am I most grateful?

Plenary/debrief

Take feedback from participants, asking them to share some of their responses. Invite others to comment, offer their appreciation for the positive and uplifting experiences shared, and their empathy and compassion for difficulties shared.

Activity 65
If/Then Intentions

Action for Happiness Key
Trying out, Direction

Individual

Rationale

Research into goal achievement suggests that setting intentions to act or behave in a particular way makes it more likely that we will do so. There are four stages which are relevant to goal achievement: predecisional, preactional, actional and postactional. Psychologists have found that we most often trip up when moving from stage 2 to stage 3 i.e. having made a decision to do something, we often find it difficult to put it into action. Gollwitzer's work (2009) suggests that if we set an 'if/then intention', i.e. 'If A happens, then I will do B', the chances of us doing what we said and achieving our goals are far higher.

Say you have a habit of nibbling unhealthy snacks in the office. Setting the following sort of if/then intention makes it more likely that you will be able to start changing that habit: If I see a packet of biscuits on Carol's desk today, then I will ignore it and walk by.

Materials

Pen and paper, happiness journal or smart phone for note-taking.

Process/procedure

1. Explain the stages in the goal-achievement process and the research behind if/then intentions. Ensure that participants understand that setting if/then intentions is about reinforcing our self-control to act in particular ways when encountering a critical situation or trigger.

2. Ask participants to think of a specific goal that they are working on at the moment, or a specific (small) problem behaviour that they want to change, for which self-control is necessary.

3. Ask each participant to create an if/then intention statement, making sure that it feels authentic.

4. If time allows, have participants share in pairs.

Plenary/debrief

Ask participants to share their goals/problem behaviour examples and their if/then intention statements. Ask each one how committed they are to their if/then intention statements on a scale of 1-10 (where 1 is not at all and 10 is fully). If less than 10/10, ask them what would increase it to 10/10.

Notes including comments and variations

If/then intentions must have the participant's commitment, hence checking whether the statement feels authentic, and whether the participant is fully committed.

In a subsequent workshop remember to ask participants how they fared with putting their if/then intentions into action. How did it support their self-control and make their goals easier to achieve?

Activity 66
Happiness Playlist

Action for Happiness Key
Emotion, Acceptance, Direction

Individual

Rationale

When we're feeling down or unhappy it's easy to become apathetic and it can be difficult to remember to do what we actually enjoy doing. This exercise is a good one to do in anticipation of one day feeling this way. By preparing our personal 'Happiness Playlist' of all the things we enjoy doing in life, not only are we boosting our mood in the moment, but we're also helping ourselves overcome negative moods that we may experience in the future. Additionally by setting an intention to use your Happiness Playlist ('If I'm feeling down or unhappy, then I will do something from my Happiness Playlist' – see previous activity), you're far more likely to use it and benefit from it.

Materials

Pen and paper, happiness journal or smart phone for note-taking. Post-it notes (see Notes below)

Process/procedure

For this exercise, simply ask participants to start a list of all the things they enjoy doing in life. It might include gardening, dancing, speaking to friends, flower-arranging, going on country walks, DIY, baking, cycling, dressing up (or dressing down), listening to music, looking through old photographs, visiting a museum or art gallery, travelling by train and so on. Michael Frisch, who introduced us to the Playlist idea, lists 221 different activities to boost your mood in his book Quality of Life Therapy (2006). Can you top that?

Plenary/debrief

Ask participants to share some of their Happiness Playlist ideas, so that other participants might be inspired ('Oh yes, I like doing that too!').

Ask them to continue adding to their lists, remembering to ask for their feedback in the next workshop.

Remind participants to enjoy the activities from their list on a regular basis.

Notes including comments and variations

This is an exercise that can be started in the workshop and continued at home. You may even like to add a competitive or collaborative element to it, i.e. see which participant can come up with the longest Happiness Playlist. You can gather in the Post-it notes after the workshop, type them up and circulate the combined Happiness Playlist to all participants.

Activity 67
Let it Flow!

Action for Happiness Key
Trying out, Direction, Emotion

Individual, pairs

Rationale

Flow (or engagement, sometimes called 'being in the zone') is the feeling of complete absorption in the moment. It is an experience that seems to be particularly common to musicians and sports people. When you are in flow time is transformed, often passing a lot more quickly than you think – before you know it, you've spent hours on something and it only seemed like minutes. One of the founding fathers of positive psychology, Professor Mihaly Csikszentmihalyi, has written extensively about flow, which is now widely accepted as a route to higher well-being. Note that the flow experience itself is not an emotional experience – in other words there is an absence of positive emotion in the moment, but we do feel good afterwards.

The flow experience occurs when certain criteria are in place, for instance, when the challenge of the task you face slightly exceeds your skill level in achieving it and when you receive moment by moment feedback on how you are doing from the task itself.

As a pathway to greater well-being, flow isn't just about feeling good after the experience has ended, it has the added benefit of stretching your capabilities as you try to meet the challenge in front of you. So there is a developmental element to flow too. This means that experiencing flow doing workplace tasks can be especially beneficial, as you're continually striving to perform better.

However, when the challenge we face far outweighs our level of skill, we usually experience anxiety and stress. And when our level of skill far outweighs the challenge, we easily get bored and apathetic. The secret seems to be getting the right balance of skill and challenge.

Materials

Pen and paper, happiness journals or smart phone for note-taking. Flip chart and pens

Process/procedure

1. Explain flow, its criteria and what it feels like. Use a simple illustration like the one below.

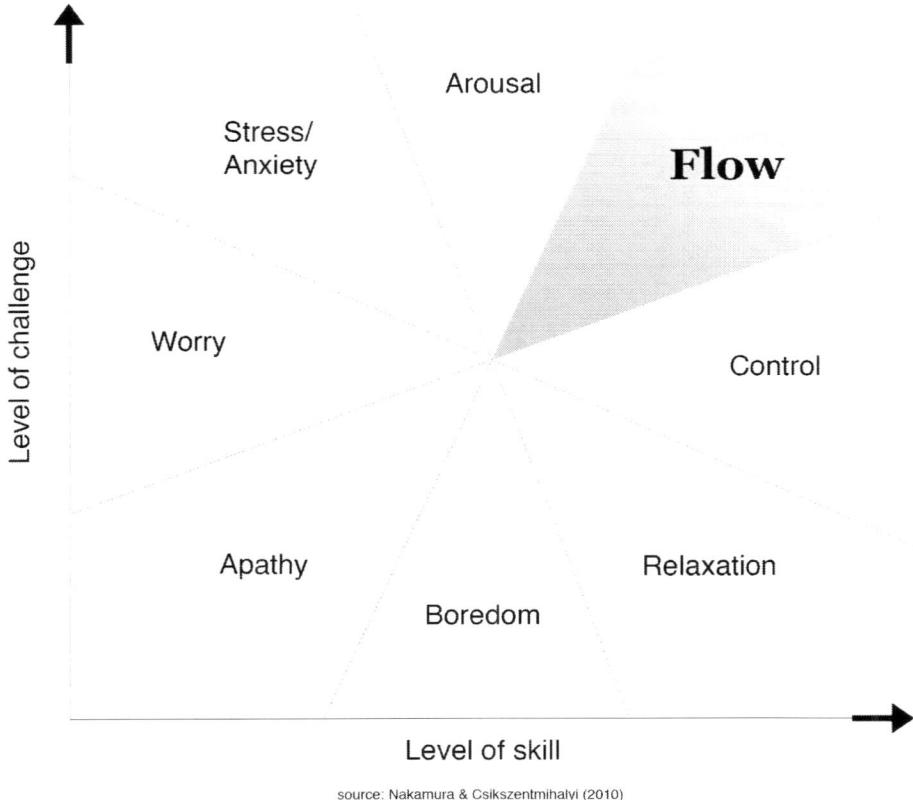

source: Nakamura & Csikszentmihalyi (2010)

2. Ask participants to list the 6-8 main tasks or activities they did this week/ this weekend. This might include things like visiting an elderly relative in hospital, playing with the kids, going to the pub with friends, chatting to a cousin in Australia on Skype, cooking the Sunday lunch, washing the car, doing some DIY, going to football or choir practice, studying at night class and so on.

3. Ask participants to draw a simple flow diagram (as above) and to decide where their main activities fit. It's unlikely that all of them will result in flow.

4. For any activities which create anxiety and stress or arousal, ask them to write down ways of a) increasing their level of skill and b) reducing the challenge of the task. If some activities result in worry, ask them to write down ways of increasing their level of skill. If some activities result in boredom, apathy or relaxation, ask them to write down ways of increasing the challenge of the task.

Plenary/debrief

Ask participants to feed back on what they have noticed about their experience of flow and to share their ideas for increasing or decreasing levels of challenge and skill. Ideas often include breaking the task down into small baby steps to decrease levels of challenge, seeking support from others and organising training, coaching or mentoring to develop ones skills.

Activity 68
Wheel of Well-being

Action for Happiness Key
Trying out, Direction, Emotion

Individual

Rationale

Martin Seligman's 'PERMA' model of well-being, described in his 2011 book, 'Flourish', gives us five different pathways to well-being: positive emotions, engagement, relationships, meaning and accomplishment. The Wheel of Well-being activity, which is based on PERMA, is a simple way to gauge your levels of well-being across those five areas, and prompts you to consider how you might increase those which are most important to you.

Materials

Handout: Wheel of Well-being. Two different colour pens/pencils per person

Handout: Wheel of Well-Being

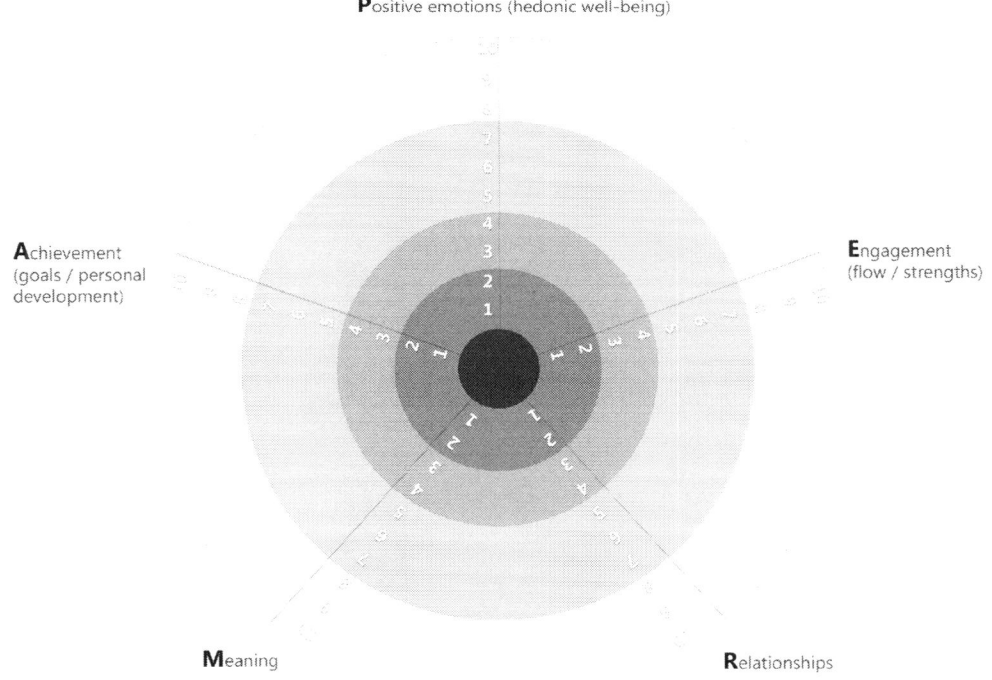

Process/procedure

1. Explain the PERMA model of well-being. For more information see chapter 2.

2. Give each participant a photocopy of the Wheel of Well-being. Ask them to consider how satisfied they are with each of the five pathways and to mark this on the handout (where 0 is not at all satisfied and 10 is very satisfied) using one colour.

3. Then ask them to consider how important each of the five pathways is to them on a scale of 0-10 (where 0 is not at all and 10 is very). Ask them to mark this on the handout using the other colour.

4. Ask them to consider any pathway where there is a gap i.e. where there is relatively low satisfaction and relatively high importance.

5. Ask participants to write down three actions they can take this week to close the gap and increase their level of satisfaction.

Plenary/debrief

Ask participants to feed back with their reflections, sharing ideas for increasing their levels of well-being in the five areas.

Notes including comments and variations

You may be asked if it's important to have a balance across the five pathways of well-being. At the moment there is no hard evidence that you do need to have a balance, or that one pathway is 'better' than another. It would seem that it very much depends on personal choice, what is most important to the individual and where you are on your life journey.

You can use this activity with any number of participants, though it is easier to discuss results in smaller groups.

Activity 69
Mental Time Travelling

Action for Happiness Key
Emotion, Relating, Appreciating

Individual, pairs

Rationale

Research suggests that reminiscing regularly about happy experiences and memories is good for your well-being, and that this can be further enhanced by recalling these happy experiences and memories in vivid detail.

Materials

Pen and paper, happiness journal or smart phone for note-taking. Participants should have somewhere quiet and comfortable to sit and relax.

Process/procedure

1. Explain to participants that practising visualising in detail the happy experiences from our past has been found to be an effective way to experience greater happiness in the present.

2. Ask participants to make a short list of their most positive memories, the happiest times that they can remember. Examples include family holidays, playing with children, celebrating a birthday or other important event etc.

3. From their list ask them to select one specific memory to focus on. When they are sitting comfortably, ask them to sit back, relax, close their eyes and bring that memory to mind. Ask them to picture the events as they happened, recalling them in as much vivid detail as they can - such as who they were with, what they did/what happened, what they were wearing at the time, what they said, the weather, the feelings they had, and so on.

4. Give them sufficient time to recall, re-experience and absorb the happy memories as they surface. Ask participants to come back to the room and open their eyes when they are ready.

5. Sharing happy memories with another person is the icing on the cake, so ask participants to pair up with someone. Give them another 5 minutes each way to exchange their stories and savour them together.

Plenary/debrief

Ask if participants want to share their happy memories with the group. If so, help them capitalise on the experience by showing genuine interest and asking questions.

Activity 70
Savouring

Action for Happiness Key
Emotion, Appreciating

Individual

Rationale

Savouring, defined as any thoughts or behaviours which generate, intensify or prolong your enjoyment, is a surprisingly effective way to increase your wellbeing. It's surprising in that it's such a simple technique, and surprising also that we don't do more of it!

Savouring is not the same as mindfulness, though there are similarities. Both techniques involve paying focussed attention, however savouring is about specifically enhancing and amplifying positive emotions related to the past, present or future, whereas the aim of mindfulness is to gain heightened awareness of the present moment (thoughts, feelings, behaviours) with open acceptance, regardless of whether the experience is good or bad.

In this activity we are savouring in the present, that is, focussing on increasing our sense of enjoyment and positive emotions in the here-and-now, using a delicious piece of fruit.

Materials

A selection of small ripe fruits (at room temperature is best) to savour, such as strawberries, raspberries and blueberries, at least one item per participant.

Process/procedure

1. Explain the process of savouring – slowing down, deliberately taking time to notice and enjoy what you're savouring, using all your senses, in this case, appreciating the fruits' scent, flavour and texture (and possibly its sound), prolonging the experience as much as you can and reflecting on your enjoyment afterwards.

2. Invite participants to select an item of fruit to savour. Have them follow the savouring process, reminding them that the point of the exercise is to eat the fruit as slowly and deliberately as possible, and enjoying it as much as possible. You might invite them to imagine that this is the very first time they have eaten a piece of fruit, or that this will be the very last time. The aim is to squeeze the maximum amount of positivity out of it. Invite them to look at their item of fruit closely first, noticing colour, texture, shape etc. Invite them to sniff the fruit before they bite into it. Ask them to bite into the fruit slowly, again noticing and enjoying the texture, flavour(s), sharpness or sweetness, softness, crunch or juiciness, and so on.

3. Do not, on any account, rush this exercise! The point is to be as slow and deliberate as possible, and to enjoy every aspect of it.

4. Ask participants to reflect on how much they enjoyed the activity.

Plenary/debrief

Invite comments from participants about what they noticed about this exercise, and what they enjoyed.

Invariably someone will comment on how different the experience of savouring is versus normal eating.

You might start a discussion about what stops us savouring food/ why we don't savour food more frequently, and what we can do to put more savouring moments into our lives.
Ask participants what else they can savour, apart from food (see below for ideas).

Notes including comments and variations

You can also invite participants to indulge in savouring at home. Savouring need not just be about food. You can savour many types of activity, such as:
- luxuriating in a warm bubble bath (the perfume, the softness, the colour and sound of the bubbles, the feel of warm water against your skin etc).
- marvelling at a beautiful sunset
- cherishing a loved one
- treasuring a childhood toy, and so on.

Activity 71
Forgiveness Letter

Action for Happiness Key
Trying Out, Emotion, Resilience

Individual

Rationale

For many people, forgiving someone is not easy. Contrary to popular belief, forgiveness is not about condoning or excusing another person's behaviour or forgetting the wrongdoing. Psychologists define forgiveness as shifting our thinking so that the wrongdoing does not loom as large, we're less focussed on retaliation and we can view it at arm's length. So, forgiveness is something we do for ourselves, not for the person who has harmed us. Forgiveness can have many positive effects on our well-being, such as reduced feelings of anger, greater optimism and better physical health. Additionally, research suggests that we're more likely to be able to forgive other people for their transgressions if we reflect first on what it feels like to be forgiven ourselves. This topic may be uncomfortable for some, so you may want to guide participants to consider only minor wrongdoings rather than major ones. Assure them that they don't have to share any details they don't want to, nor, having written a forgiveness letter, do they send it. The purpose of the exercise is to benefit the forgiver, not the person being forgiven.

Materials

Pen and paper, happiness journal or smart phone for making notes.

Process/procedure

1. Set the scene by explaining the research behind forgiveness. You might start the exercise by asking participants to work in pairs, reflecting on a time when they held a grudge against someone for a small misdemeanour. Perhaps they can think of an occasion from the school playground. Ask them to consider how it felt to hold the grudge (good and bad) and what happened to their relationship as a result.

2. Next invite participants to consider a time when they themselves have been forgiven for a minor wrong doing. Ask them to reflect on how that felt, and what happened to the relationship as a result.

3. Ask participants to take a piece of paper and draft a forgiveness letter to someone who has hurt them in some way. Ask them to describe:
   a. the wrongdoing
   b. how it affected them at the time
   c. what they would have liked the person to have done.

4. Finish the letter with a short statement of forgiveness and understanding.

5. Make sure participants are aware that the letter is for their benefit only, and not to be sent.

Plenary/debrief

Invite comments and observations about how it felt to write the letter. Remind participants that writing the letter is solely for their benefit and not to be sent. Remind them that they do not have to share the details of their letter or the original wrong-doing itself. Some participants may find this exercise too hard to do in the workshop, so remind them that forgiveness is a skill that they can acquire with practice.

Activity 72
How Flexible is Your Thinking?

Action for Happiness Key
Trying out, Resilience

Small groups

Rationale

Carol Dweck's ground-breaking research on mindsets forms a fundamental building block in helping people understand that, even if they are stuck in a negative way of thinking, it is possible to change. Essentially, Dweck found that some people believe that intelligence and other abilities (such as artistic, sporting, musical) are carved in stone – you're either born with them or you're not – this is what she calls a 'fixed mindset'.

There are a number of negative consequences to having a fixed mindset, such as seeing failure as a result of lack of intelligence rather than lack of effort, responding in a helpless way to failure, and not making an effort. People with a fixed mindset do not respond well to failure, believing that it reflects badly on them and highlights a lack of innate ability. Since they believe that ability is innate and cannot be developed, they do not try.

Positive psychology research suggests that people who have a flexible (or 'growth') mindset (i.e. they believe that intelligence and ability can develop with effort) are more likely to make an effort when things don't go according to plan, are more resilient when faced with set-backs or failure, and have higher well-being.

Learning about mindsets and how the brain develops as we learn new things, and praising for effort rather than for ability all help to develop a flexible growth mindset.

Materials

Pen and paper, happiness journal or smart phone for making notes.

Several questions on different aspects of mindsets, at least one per group, for example:
- Imagine you are a hard-working employee who has been passed over for promotion. How would you feel about this if you have a 'fixed' mindset? What kind of things might you think and how would you behave? How would it be different if you had a 'growth' mindset?
- Do you know anyone (friend, family, colleague) who has a fixed mindset? Can you think of an example of when you have noticed their fixed mindset? What might you do to help them develop a flexible mindset?
- How might someone with a fixed mindset feel about failing an exam? What problems might a fixed mindset cause them? What are the advantages of developing a flexible (growth) mindset?
- Can you name some famous people with an obvious fixed or flexible mindset? What do they do/how do they behave which makes you think this?
- Depending on who your participants are (age, experience, gender etc.) you can create your own mindset questions to suit.

Process/procedure

1. Explain the difference between fixed and flexible mindsets. Ask participants which mindset most resonates with them. Note that mindsets are domain-specific so it's highly unlikely that anyone has a fixed or flexible mindset about everything in their life.

2. Depending on the number of participants, divide them into groups of 3-5 and give each group a mindset question to consider. Ask them to summarise their discussion and their learning points for the plenary.

Plenary/debrief

Go round each group, asking someone to read their question set and their responses. Invite other groups to respond.

Lead a general discussion about fixed/flexible mindsets, with personal examples if possible. Ensure you include a discussion about the relative merits of both mindsets.

Ask what actions participants might now take to ensure that they notice their mindset and try to respond more frequently with a flexible mindset, if this is not their natural style.

Notes including comments and variations

If you're running short of time and you're working with a small group (10 or fewer), you can divide them into two groups, give them the same question set, and have one group work on the responses from a fixed mindset perspective and the other from a growth mindset perspective, before leading a whole group discussion.

Activity 73
Counting Kindnesses

Action for Happiness Key
Appreciating, Emotion

Individual

Rationale

Everyone working the field of positive psychology will have heard of the 'Three Good Things' exercise, sometimes known as 'counting your blessings'. In this version, we focus on counting the kind events or experiences in our lives. It's another way of overcoming the negativity bias and refocusing our attention on the positive things that we already have in our lives.

Materials

Pen and paper, happiness journal or smart phone for making notes.

Process/procedure

1. Explain that the activity is about spotting the examples of kindness that we readily experience every day, but either don't register or forget about very quickly.

2. Ask each person to think back over the past 24 hours and to jot down as many examples of kind acts that they have witnessed, or have done themselves. Examples might be seeing someone help a fellow commuter on the tube, a passenger giving up a seat for another person, someone putting money in a busker's hat or charity tin; children packing shopping at the checkout for charity, and so on.

Plenary/debrief

Ask for comments and observations. It is likely that someone will offer the observation that there are far more kind deeds being done than we think, even in very busy places like big cities where we tend to think people are less friendly.

Notes including comments and variations

Ask participants to consciously notice kind acts between now and their next workshop, to keep a note and to bring this with them next time. Be sure to take feedback on this when you next see them.

Activity 74
Treasure Chest

Action for Happiness Key
Emotion

Individual

Rationale

This is a wonderful activity devised by Barbara Fredrickson (an expert on positive emotions) which can boost your mood as you do it and also when you come back to it in the future.

The idea is very simply to collect together some examples of things which lift your spirits, such as photos of loved ones, holiday snaps, certificates of examination grades or other achievements, sporting trophies, love letters or valentines cards, thank you letters, pictures that your kids have drawn, models that they have made at school, recordings of special songs and so on. You can choose a beautiful box or chest to keep tangible items in, and/or you can take photos of the items on your phone so that you have a portable treasure chest.

Every time you need an emotional lift you just peek inside the chest.

Materials

Pen and paper, happiness journal or smart phone on which to make initial notes. Each participant needs to select a box (which they can decorate) or chest in which to keep their 'treasure', and/or record each item in the box on their smart phone.

Process/procedure

1. Explain the idea of keeping a treasure chest of special items which boost your mood. Ask participants to start making a list of all the things they will put in their box when they get home.

2. Ensure they know that they can keep a 'virtual' treasure chest as well / instead if they prefer.

3. Ask participants to start creating their treasure chest at home and if practical, to bring them to your next workshop to discuss.

Plenary/debrief

None required.

Notes including comments and variations

Fredrickson suggests that you can create different types of 'positivity portfolios' to create different moods. For example, you could create different portfolios specifically to inspire the positive feelings of confidence, pride, amusement, joy and so on.

Activity 75
Humour Diary

Action for Happiness Key
Emotion, Appreciating

Individual

Rationale

This is a variation on the Gratitude Diary, and is based on preliminary research conducted by humour expert, Professor Willibald Ruch at the University of Zurich. It suggests that it's possible to alleviate bad moods and improve good moods by consciously noticing the funny things that happen in your life.

Materials

Pen and paper, happiness journal or smart phone for note taking.

Process/procedure

1. Explain the idea of the gratitude diary if participants are unaware of it, and that this activity is a variation on that theme.

2. Ask participants to reflect for a few minutes on what has happened to them over the course of the past 24-48 hours and to try to remember all the humorous things that happened. Since humour is very personal, what one person will find funny may not work for someone else.

3. If this is difficult for people, ask them to record times when they saw and/or heard someone laugh, and if possible to write down the cause. Those with children may find this easier.

Plenary/debrief

Ask people for their comments and observations on this exercise, and to share some of their amusing incidents with the group (if <12) or with a partner (if >12). Ask them to continue recording funny incidents regularly for the next week, or until you see them at the next workshop.

Notes including comments and variations

Ensure that you debrief people on their humour diaries again at the following workshop.

Activity 76
Disputing Negative Thoughts

Action for Happiness Key
Resilience, Trying out, Emotion

Individual

Rationale

According to Professor Martin Seligman at the University of Pennsylvania, the ability to dispute our automatic negative thoughts is vital in order to develop the everyday resilience to cope with adversity and disappointment, and to change from a pessimistic way of explaining what happens to us to a more optimistic way. Note that Seligman does not mean 'blind optimism' where you try to think positively about absolutely everything in every circumstance, but 'realistic optimism', which means taking an optimistic outlook where one is warranted.

Being able to dispute negative thoughts requires that you first understand the well-known 'ABC' technique of Cognitive Behavioural Therapy (CBT), where A stands for 'adversity', B stands for 'belief' and C stands for 'consequence'. Having identified the ABCs of a specific situation, you then move on to dispute (D) your negative beliefs. Successful disputation is followed by a feeling of renewed vigour or energy, so the whole process is often referred to as 'ABCDE':

Adversity > Belief > Consequence > Disputation > Energisation.

Materials

Pen and paper, happiness journal or smart phone for note-taking. Flip chart and flip chart pens.

Process/procedure

1. Explain the ABC technique on which CBT is based. Essentially what CBT has taught us is that it is not the adversity (A) itself that causes the negative consequences (C) for our emotions and behaviours, but the beliefs (B) that we hold about the adversity.

2. Draw up an ABCDE framework on the flip chart (or a couple if you are going to talk through an example) – see overleaf.

3. You might choose to provide a simple example, such as how an adversity like being late for work (A) causes us to feel stressed and anxious (the emotional consequences element of C) and (assuming we are usually a considerate driver!) to drive aggressively, swear at other drivers, queue-jump, park in a visitor's space, stomp into the office and shout at our colleagues (the behavioural consequences part of C). CBT tells us that it is the beliefs (B) we hold about A which lead to C. Note that in this activity by 'beliefs' we mean our instantaneous or automatic negative thoughts about the adversity, not our deeply-rooted or long-held beliefs. In this case you might think that you'll look inefficient, disorganised and unprofessional for being late to work or that colleagues will think you don't take your work seriously, and so on.

ABCDE Framework

A		
Adversity		
B	**C**	**D**
Beliefs	Consequences	Disputation
E		
Energisation (new, more positive emotions and behaviour)		

4. Using a new flip chart page, ask the participants to suggest another minor adversity. Write this up as the 'A'.

5. Ask participants to suggest possible consequences (C) for your emotions and behaviour of this adversity, and write them in the appropriate column on the flip chart. It is sometimes easier to work from A to C then back to B, because the Cs are often more obvious.

6. Then ask participants to think of some possible beliefs (B) and write them up on the flip chart. Sometimes at this stage participants are still thinking of consequences, so ensure that you put Bs and Cs in the correct column.

7. Having thought of at least three possible Bs and Cs, ask participants to dispute the Bs one by one, that is, to think of ways of challenging or arguing against each B. There are at least 4 different ways to dispute a negative thought, which are:
> i. using evidence to test the belief. Try to complete the sentence 'This belief isn't completely true because...'
> ii. generating a more positive alternative belief. Try to complete the sentence 'Another way I can look at this is...'
> iii. putting it into perspective. Try to complete the sentence 'The most likely cause is..... And that means I can .....'
> iv. testing its usefulness. Ask 'Which explanation is most useful to me in terms of maintaining a positive mood and achieving my goals?'

8. Try using one of these sentence completion tasks to dispute the possible beliefs. Some may work better than others. Write these in the D column

9. Having successful disputed the Bs, you can discuss how this might result in different, more positive, consequences (C) for mood and behaviour. Ask whether energisation (E) would occur as a result.

Plenary/debrief
None required.

Notes including comments and variations

If you choose to have participants work through the ABCDE technique using their own adversity, ask them to choose a minor one, or one that has already been successfully dealt with and is no longer an issue for them.

Ask participants to try disputing their automatic negative thoughts over the course of the coming week, and to report back next time on the difference it makes to their feelings and behaviours.

Activity 77
Resilience Timeline

Action for Happiness Key
Resilience, Trying out, Acceptance

Individual

Rationale

It is a common misconception that true resilience is the domain of extraordinary people, the types of people who survive exceptional challenges or disasters that are featured in the news. Yet all of us are resilient in some way, and will have successfully come through adversity or disappointment in the past. This is why psychologist Ann Masten refers to psychological resilience as 'ordinary magic'.

This activity requires participants to reflect on their lives in a visual way, and to notice how they have successfully come through adversities in the past.

This might be a challenging exercise for people who are facing current adversities, so you need to be sensitive to that possibility

Materials

Pen and paper on which to draw a personal timeline .Flip chart and flip chart pens on which to draw an example timeline (see below).

Process/procedure

1. Explain that we will all have come through adversities during our lives. Whether we classify a negative event or experience as an adversity depends on the individual. The same is true of positive events. For some people, it may be a triumph to walk to the shops once a week, or to talk to neighbours.

2. Using the flip chart, draw a timeline template in the shape of a capital T on its side, with time shown along the horizontal axis, positive at the top of the vertical axis and negative at the bottom.

3. Then plot an imaginary timeline, or one of someone you know (ensuring that they cannot be identified), showing the highs and lows of this person's life over the years. Lows may include adversities such as failing exams, being expelled from school, getting divorced, losing a job and so on. You can also include specific events as 'highs', however in our experience it is helpful just to show that a person does bounce back from adversities, given time and support.

4. Ask participants to plot their own resilience timeline, reflect on how they have come through various negative events and experiences, and to consider what has been helpful in doing so.

Plenary/debrief

None required.

Activity 78
Appreciating Our Relationships

Action for Happiness Key
Relating, Emotion, Trying out, Meaning

Pairs

Rationale

Although Appreciative Inquiry (Cooperrider & Shrivastva, 1987) predates the arrival of positive psychology by a good 10 years, its principles are an excellent fit. The Appreciative Inquiry (AI) process is most often used in organisational settings, however, it can be adapted for more personal use, as shown in the following activity.

Materials

Pen and paper, happiness journal or smart phone for note-taking.

Handout of AI questions such as:
- What is it that you value most in the other person?
- What do you value most about the relationship you have together?
- Throughout your relationship you will have had ups and downs, high points and low points. Think back to a high point, a time that stands out as a great period or experience in your relationship. What was that time and what it was that made it such a high point for you?
- As you think about your relationship overall, the good times and the difficult times, what do you think is at the foundation of your relationship? What is it about this relationship that makes it really work? Give some examples.
- What are some of the things that you do well together?
- What three wishes would you make to heighten the vitality and health of your relationship?

Process/procedure

1. Ask participants to select a strong, current relationship to reflect on (this could be a sibling, a work colleague, a friend etc.) and to work in pairs.

2. Give each participant a handout of AI-based questions and ask them to take 10 minutes each way (more if you have the time) to answer whichever questions resonate most with them.

Plenary/debrief

Take feedback from participants, focusing on the positive emotions that arise.

Activity 79
Strengths Spotting

Action for Happiness Key
***Emotion, Trying out,
Acceptance, Relating***

Pairs

Rationale

Personal strengths are a cornerstone of positive psychology. There are currently four psychometrically-tested strengths models, the Clifton StrengthsFinder™, Strengthscope™, VIA and Realise2. In the course of the research which led to the creation of the Realise2 strengths model, Professor Alex Linley at the Centre for Applied Positive Psychology in the UK identified a number of key areas which give us clues about our natural strengths. The strengths spotting questions in this exercise are based on that work.

The activity requires you to work in pairs, 'spotting' each others strengths through a series of simple coaching questions.

Materials

Pen and paper, happiness journal or smart phone for note-taking.

Process/procedure

1. Ask participants to work in pairs, co-coaching using any of the following questions. They do not have to use them all, just the ones which appeal most. Allow them about 15 minutes each way.
    i. What are you doing when you are at your best?
    ii. What do you find easy to do? What are you naturally good at?
    iii. What energizes you?
    iv. What skill(s) do you pick up quickly and easily?
    v. What sort of thing do you do just for the love of it?
    vi. What are you naturally interested in or attracted by?
    vii. What really motivates you?
    viii. What activities give you flow (where you're completely absorbed and lose track of time)?
    ix. What are you really passionate about?
    x. What were you good at as a child and how does this show up in your life now?

2. Ask them to make a few notes on what they have discovered about their strengths.

Plenary/debrief

Take feedback from participants. It may be that some have discovered strengths that they didn't know they had, or have had the existence of a strength confirmed. Could they use some of the questions with family, friends or colleagues?

Activity 80
Family Strengths Tree

Action for Happiness Key
Relating, Emotion, Trying out

Individual

Rationale

Having identified and worked on our personal strengths in various activities in this book, it is very helpful to broaden our thinking about strengths to include family members.

This is a particularly helpful activity for building stronger bonds between family members, especially where there may be a tendency to focus on weaknesses or on what others don't do well. It makes a refreshing change and helps you to see others in a new, more positive light.

Materials

Pen and paper, happiness journal or smart phone on which to draw a family tree. List of the 24 VIA strengths on a handout or slide as a prompt

Process/procedure

1. Ask participants to draw a simple family tree on a piece of paper. This might take the form of a traditional family tree showing generations and lines of marriage and birth or it may look more like a mind map. Ask them to identify the people in their family that are important to them. They can include some people and leave out others, it's up to each individual.

2. For each person they have listed on their family tree/mind map, ask them to identify up to three strengths, which they should write next to that person's name. If they don't know what their strengths are, they can make a best guess. They may use strengths from the VIA assessment (have a copy on a handout or slide for participants to refer to), or ones which they have observed (such as the strengths revealed through the previous strengths spotting exercise).

3. Once they have identified up to three strengths per person, encourage them to add more family members, perhaps those who are not so close, and to identify their strengths.

Plenary/debrief

Ask participants to feedback on the process. Some participants may comment on the fact that it makes them see someone in a new light. Others may comment that it's not easy to do, even with people you have known for years, as there is a tendency for negative labels to stick.

Activity 81
Resilience Hero

Action for Happiness Key
Resilience, Trying out, Acceptance, Emotion, Meaning

Individual

Rationale

Albert Bandura's research (1997) on developing self-efficacy suggests that one of the most effective ways is to model other people's behaviour that you want to adopt for yourself. This activity involves identifying someone who displays the kind of resilient behaviour that you would like to have. Your 'resilience hero' might be someone in your family, a friend or colleague, or someone you have heard about in the media.

Materials

Pen and paper, happiness journal or smart phone for note-taking. Flip chart and pens.

Process/procedure

1. Explain that sometimes it easy to see in other people the kinds of the behaviour we'd like to have ourselves, and that one way of developing new behaviours is to model what we see other people doing.

2. Ask each participant to spend 3-4 mins identifying someone who could act as their 'resilience hero', i.e. someone who doesn't let life's knocks and setbacks get them down, or someone who has bounced back from adversity. This may be someone they know well, or someone they have come across in the media.

3. Ask them to identify the behaviours that this person shows. Perhaps they can retell a story about the person, the hardship they have suffered and how they responded to it.

4. The key to this activity is to try to identify what this person does and the kind of thoughts that they might have which enable them to be resilient, so that they might be modelled. If participants aren't sure, ask them to make their best guess.

5. Ask participants to consider the following questions:
    - What happened?
    - What strengths did/does the person show?
    - What did they do which helped them overcome the adversity?
    - What can you learn from their behaviour?

Plenary/debrief

Encourage participants to share their resilience hero stories and talk through their responses to the above questions. In terms of actions to help overcome the adversity, they might consider practical actions as well as new thinking, and possibly the creation of new meaning.

Summarise their learning points on a flip chart and encourage participants to put them into action within the next 48 hours.

Activity 82
Open Doors

Action for Happiness Key
Resilience, Trying out, Emotion, Meaning Appreciating

Pairs

Rationale

Tayyab Rashid is one of the world's leading experts on applying positive psychology in therapeutic settings. This activity, which takes the 'Resilience Timeline' activity one stage further, encourages participants to reconsider negative experiences and events in their lives from a new perspective, identifying any new doors that have opened for them as a result of old ones closing.

Materials

Pen and paper, happiness journal or smart phone for note-taking.

Process/procedure

1. Explain that sometimes new opportunities arise only because of negative events or experiences. One frequent example is when redundancy leads a person to retrain in a new field and find a job that makes them feel happier and more fulfilled than they were previously.

2. Working in pairs, ask participants to reflect on some of their own adversities and try to identify any new doors which opened as a result.

3. Rashid also suggests reflecting on what gets in the way of your ability to see these open doors and what you can do in the future to find them more readily.

Plenary/debrief

Ask participants to share with the group any examples that they have from their own lives.

- What enhances our ability to see open doors and walk through them?
- What prevents us from seeing open doors?

Notes including comments and variations

This exercise is harder than it appears. It's very easy to reframe negative situations in a mechanistic way, but to make a difference it must be meaningful to the person concerned.

Activity 83
Vital Friends

Action for Happiness Key
Relating, Trying out

Individual

Rationale

In studies based on work-places in the US, one of the most important factors explaining what engages people is whether or not they have a best friend at work. As a result of working with the Gallup Organisation on employee engagement, Tom Rath began studying friendship, identifying eight key roles that friends play in our lives.

This activity encourages us to identify and value the role(s) that our friends play in our lives, as well as consider the role(s) that we play for them.

Materials

Pen and paper, happiness journal or smart phone for note-taking. A handout outlining Tom Rath's eight vital friendship roles

Process/procedure

1. Talk through Tom Rath's eight Vital Friendship roles:
   - *Builder* – a great motivator. The builder invests time in helping you develop, they don't compete with you
   - *Champion* – a personal promoter. The champion sings your praises even when you're not around
   - *Collaborator* – relates to your passions. They have similar interests and ambitions
   - *Companion* – always there for you in good times and bad
   - *Connector* – helps you get what you want e.g. by introducing you to others
   - *Energiser* – a 'fun' friend who always gives you a boost and helps you relax
   - *Mind-Opener* – expands your horizons and encourages you to embrace new ideas and opportunities
   - *Navigator* – guides and advises you, and keeps you heading in the right direction

2. Ask participants to draw a simple mind map of their current relationships, including family, friends, colleagues and other acquaintances. Have them select 3-5 friends, and identify what role(s) they play, with examples if possible. Ask them to reflect on the significance of thinking of their friends in this way.

Plenary/debrief

Encourage participants to ask friends what role they play for them: they may be surprised!

Activity 84
Aims and Guidelines

Action for Happiness Key
Direction, Trying out

Individual

Rationale

The purpose of this activity is to clarify your aims, as facilitator, for this workshop. It will also help participants clarify their own aims, and help them prepare themselves to get the most out of the workshop.

Materials

Handout: Aims and Guidelines for Getting the Most out of this Workshop.

Process/procedure

1. Prepare a handout with your aims for the workshop – and modify the guidelines in whatever ways you think are appropriate for your workshop and your facilitator style.

2. Distribute the handout and go over your aims. Then allow participants time to respond and complete the part listing their own particular aims for the workshop.

3. Explain the part of the handout which says 'The keys to getting most out of a workshop as a participant are…:'. Briefly explain that long experience with workshops suggests that these really are the keys and briefly elaborate on the meaning of each one, possibly with an example of each in the context of workshop participation. Then suggest that half-way through the workshop (i.e. at the lunchtime for a one-day workshop) each participant scores themselves on how well they are doing against each of the keys.

Plenary/debrief

Give the participants an opportunity to respond and negotiate any changes as required.

Ask the participants about how well, in their experience, the 'keys to getting the most of a workshop' also apply to life more generally?

Handout: Aims and Guidelines for Getting the Most from this Workshop

The facilitator's aims for this workshop are:	My own personal aims for this workshop are:
1.	1.
2.	2.
3.	3.
4.	4.

The keys to getting most out of a workshop as a participant are:

	Self-assessment (score out of 10)
PARTICIPATION	
EXPERIMENTATION	
REFLECTION	
CONTRIBUTION	

Workshops Guidelines

We will take breaks but feel free to take care of your own personal needs without waiting for a formal break.

Be as open as you can be but you have a right to your privacy and to pass when you choose.

Make at least one new acquaintance today – someone you will contact afterwards.

Activity 85
Just Walking

Action for Happiness Key
Relating, Trying out, Emotion, Exercise

Individual, pairs

Rationale

This activity is a great ice-breaker to run at the beginning of a happiness workshop because it starts the process of getting participants acquainted with each other – they have to connect with at least one other person. They will also need to make eye contact with each other. In addition, it gives participants an opportunity to express their gratitude and to be thanked. In fact, it addresses the first five of the Action for Happiness keys to happiness in a very mild way. It's a sort of 'happiness-lite'.

Materials

None required.

Process/procedure

1. Introduce the activity as an ice-breaker, a way of testing the effect of having happy thoughts and starting to get to know some other participants in the workshop.

2. Say that the first part of this activity is to just walk around the room in a happy way. You may find it helpful to think a happy thought as you do so – e.g. you might think about someone you care about, a happy memory or something you're looking forward to ... or you can just fake it - that's fine too. Demonstrate how you would do this but emphasise that everyone will have their own way of doing it.

3. After 1 minute ask participants to now start acknowledging other people as they pass them e.g. by a smile or a nod or in any other way i.e. express some form of non-verbal greeting.

4. After another minute, ask participants to take the hand of someone they don't know and walk with them as a pair. If some participants look as if they might find this difficult you can remind them that they probably learned how to do this in kindergarten! Again, acknowledge other pairs non-verbally as you pass them.

5. After another minute, ask participants to thank their partners for accompanying them ... in whatever way they feel is appropriate.

Plenary/debrief

Who found that easy?   ... did anyone find it difficult? If anyone says they did find it difficult then say it is probably the most challenging thing they will be asked to do in the workshop (if it is!).

You could use the plenary of this activity to introduce the first five of the Action for Happiness Keys to Happiness.

Notes including comments and variations

Variations – you could play some up-beat music during each of the one minute periods ... this will give a common rhythm to the participants which will help build connection.

You could suggest that participants experiment with different kinds of smile or nod or other form of non-verbal greeting in stage two – or you could introduce an extra stage for this.

Note that this activity addresses the first five keys to happiness of Action for Happiness's Keys to Happiness, but in a very light way:

- *Giving*: participants give acknowledgement to other participants and give thanks to their partner at the end.
- *Relating*: participants relate to other participants as they walk, and to their partner in the final stage.
- *Exercise*: walking is exercise.
- *Appreciating*: participants are appreciating their own happiness by walking in a happy way, they are appreciating each other as they greet them non-verbally and they express their appreciation of their partner when they thank them at the end.
- *Trying out*: this activity involved people doing something new – or perhaps something they haven't done since kindergarten i.e. holding hands with a stranger as you walk together.

Activity 86
Human Bingo

Action for Happiness Key
Emotion, Relating

Individual, groups

Rationale

In order for participants to relax and feel comfortable experimenting with new ideas, they have to feel comfortable with themselves and with each other. It's unlikely that they all know each other well already so this exercise is about getting them better acquainted and letting them know that there will be a 'fun' element to this workshop. It's an ideal exercise to run as an ice-breaker at the start of the workshop; it's not too taxing, but it's purposeful and lots of fun. Following this activity, people will feel much more relaxed and able to participate fully in the workshop.

Materials

Handout: Human Bingo.

Process/procedure

1. Tell the participants it's time to play 'a nice game of bingo'. You might have to explain how bingo works if participants are not familiar with this game. Distribute copies of the bingo 'card'.

2. Each person must get up, move around the room, and find someone who fits a particular blank on the card. They must ask their name and write in that particular slot. For example if Amy Simpson has been to the loo in the Louvre you would write her name in the box for that item on the bingo card.

3. The first person to get a full line - horizontal, vertical or diagonal - call out 'bingo'!!!!

Important: No-one can have their name against more than one item on a card even though they may qualify for more than one category.

Note: tell the group they can be as creative as they want in finding people for their categories.

Plenary/debrief

None required.

Handout: Human Bingo

Find someone who...

Has given up smoking (and not started again!)	Plays a musical instrument	Won a prize at school	Can roller skate or roller blade	Has been to the London Eye
Has climbed a mountain	Can whistle (what?)	Has seen a dolphin in the wild	Has been to the loo in the Louvre	Has exhibited paintings
Passed their driving test first time	Has been cycling in a foreign country	Can juggle	Has performed on stage	Has sung in a choir
Can row a boat	Exercises regularly	Has held a snake	Can stand on their head	Has won a fancy dress competition

Activity 87
People Hunting

Action for Happiness Key
Emotion, Relating

Individual and small groups

Rationale

In order for participants to relax and feel comfortable experimenting with new ideas, they have to feel comfortable with themselves and with each other. It's unlikely that they all know each other well already so this exercise is about getting them better acquainted and letting them know that there will be a 'fun' element to this workshop. It's an ideal exercise to run as an ice-breaker at the start of the workshop; it's not too taxing, but it's purposeful and lots of fun. Following this activity, people will feel much more relaxed and able to participate fully in the workshop.

Materials

If there are more than about 30 people then it will be helpful to have a hand mic.

Pencils or pens.

A sheet of paper with about a dozen of the items listed below. (Cards would be better as they are easier to write on but more difficult to prepare).

Process/procedure

1. Introduce the activity by explaining its purpose and distributing the sheets. Give the participants a short while to read the items. You could say something like:
   > *'The purpose of this activity is to get acquainted with some other people here who you don't already know. Try to match people with the items on the list on your sheet (or card). Put their first name against each of the items. You've got 20 minutes to meet a range of other people starting from now.'*

You might wish to suggest a target number of people to talk to, or a minimum number.

2. Every few minutes or so remind the participants they should be moving on to meet other participants.

3. After about 20 minutes, ask them to return to their seats.

Plenary/debrief

Use the following to help participants process the experience:

- What was the most interesting bit of information you learned about another participant?

- Which information was easiest and which was hardest to give to another participant?

- How do we help ourselves and others become comfortable more quickly when we are in a new group of people?

Notes including comments and variations

This activity is best with at least a dozen people – and can be used with up to a hundred people.

Allow about 2-3 minutes for instructions and 20-25 for milling about – but allow significantly more time if it is to be followed by small group discussion (see above).

You can give people the handout sheets (or cards) when they first arrive to register at the workshop so they can start mingling and having conversations straight away.

Suggest participants retain the names of the people they met in this activity and resolve to meet up again during any breaks or after the session to continue their conversations.

When the time for mingling is up, ask the participants to form small groups to process the experience. Have them discuss the debrief questions together.

People Hunting Examples

Here are a range of items you could use or adapt to match the aims of your workshop. Use about a dozen items and certainly not more than 15:

Find someone who:

- can name a hero or heroine who has been a role model for them
- shares the same hobby as you do
- shares the same astrological sign as you do
- is feeling great
- has given up a habit recently
- has had a success recently
- has a favourite saying that guides their decision-making
- enjoys leadership
- has heard a joke recently and is willing to share it
- took a risk this past week
- travelled furthest to get here

- has a tip on managing stress
- carries at least 8 membership cards
- is not sure why s/he is here today
- is sure why s/he is here today
- needs a 'shot in the arm'
- has blue eyes
- needs a backrub
- had a 'first' this year
- had a child born or adopted into his/her family this year
- had a child move out this year
- was born in the same city or town as you
- has written a book
- talks to his/her houseplants
- has had a conflict already today.
- enjoys speaking in public

Alternatively, you could just use items that relate to some of the '10 Keys' to Happiness of Action for Happiness. For example:

Find someone who:
- has bought a 'Big Issue' in the last month
- is feeling great today
- takes exercise regularly
- took a risk this past week
- has had a success recently
- can name a teacher to whom they are really grateful
- is in love with someone

- has given up a habit recently
- has heard a joke recently and is willing to share it
- is clear about their purpose in life

Another option is to use items that help people find others who have things in common with them. For example:

Find someone who:

- shares the same hobby as you do
- shares the same astrological sign as you do
- has the same colour eyes
- has the same favourite colour
- has the same favourite food
- has the same favourite flower
- has been on holiday to the same place as you
- likes the same kinds of films
- likes the same kind of music that you do

As another alternative, you could mix the last two categories (i.e. the Action for Happiness keys and things in common). For example:

Find someone who:

- is feeling great
- has bought a "Big Issue' in the last month
- is clear about their purpose in life
- took a risk this past week
- has given up a habit recently
- likes the same kind of music that you do
- shares the same astrological sign as you do
- has been on holiday to the same place as you

Activity 88
A Few Things about Me

Action for Happiness Key
Emotion, Acceptance, Relating, Direction

Individual, small groups

Rationale

In order for participants to relax and feel comfortable experimenting with new ideas, they have to feel comfortable with themselves and with each other. It's unlikely that they all know each other well already so this exercise is about getting them better acquainted and letting them know that there will be a 'fun' element to this workshop. It's an ideal exercise to run as an ice-breaker at the start of the workshop; it's not too taxing, but it's purposeful and lots of fun. Following this activity, people will feel much more relaxed and able to participate fully in the workshop.

Materials

Handout: A Few things about Me.

Process/procedure

1. Explain the purpose of this activity and distribute the handout below.

2. Let the participants have about 3-5 minutes to fill out the handout individually.

3. Form small groups of about three to five people and ask them to share their responses to one of the items they've answered on the handout.

4. Reassemble the whole group and ask for volunteers to share any patterns of information the small groups discovered about themselves.

Plenary/debrief

Try to relate some of the observations from stage 4 above to the objectives of your happiness workshop.

Handout: A Few Things About Me

Please take 4 or 5 minutes to respond briefly to the following statements.

Shortly, you'll be asked to share some of your responses with your group as a way of getting to know each other a little better:

List two things that are really important to you:

    1.

    2.

List two things that you've done that you are proud of:

    1.

    2.

List two things you would like to accomplish during the next three years:

    1.

    2.

Activity 89
Letter to Self

Action for Happiness Key
Direction, Trying out

Individual

Rationale
This is a traditional workshop activity to encourage participants to turn their learning and their good intentions into actions. It will also help reinforce some of the lessons from the workshop and strengthen the determination of the participants to take action to live a happier life.

Materials
Paper, pen and envelope for each participant.

Process/procedure
1. Hand out the stationery to each participant.

2. Ask participants to address an envelope to themselves.

3. Ask the participants to write a letter to themselves about the changes they want to make in their lives as a result of participating in the workshop to live happier lives. Ask them to make a note in the letter of their most important goal.

4. Then ask them to put their letter in an envelope and seal it.

5. Collect in the letters.

6. Mail the letters to the participants one week after the workshop.

Plenary/debrief
What kind of changes did participants write about?

What were the main goals they identified?

Notes including comments and variations
If running the workshop in parts, at the next one you might ask participants to feed back on how motivating it felt to receive and read the letter they wrote.

Activity 90
Stop, Start and Continue

Action for Happiness Key
Direction, Trying out

Individual

Rationale

If participants don't do anything with what they learned from the workshop then it is not likely to have much effect on their sustainable happiness. The objective of this exercise therefore is to turn the lessons from the workshop into actions and to strengthen the participants' determination to take action to live a happier life.

Materials

Handout: STOP, START and CONTINUE

Process/procedure

1. Introduce the activity by emphasising the importance of new actions and new behaviours in reaching new levels of happiness. Possibly mention the catchy words: 'If you always do what you've always done, then you'll always get what you've always got.'

2. Give each participant a 'STOP, START and CONTINUE' handout (see below).

3. Remind participants about the ground covered in the workshop by conducting a brainstorm on 'What have we done in this workshop – what can you remember?'

4. Then do a round of participants' learning points from the workshop. You may wish to display the following 'stems' for participants to use:
   - I learned...
   - I relearned...
   - I discovered that...
   - I was surprised that...
   - I noticed that...

5. Ask participants to complete their STOP, START and CONTINUE handout.

6. Do a round in which each participant shares one item from their STOP, START and CONTINUE handout.

Plenary/debrief

None required.

Handout: Stop, Start and Continue

After today...

STOP: One thing I'm going to stop doing (or do less of):

START: One thing I'm going to start doing (or do more of):

CONTINUE: One thing I'm going to do carry on doing because it works for me:

Activity 91
Simple Feedback Form

Action for Happiness Key
Giving, Appreciating

Individual

Rationale

Feedback forms at the end of workshops are sometimes, rather sceptically, called 'Happy Sheets' and it does seem to be the case that most participants express greater satisfaction with a workshop at the end of it when they are still there than a few days later.

Nevertheless, it can be very helpful to get feedback from participants at the end of the workshop to help improve subsequent workshops. And it's good to know where you were on-target as well as where there are opportunities for improvement.

Moreover, if you are going to use a feedback form, it makes sense to use one that will help the participants do some learning along the way. Here is an example of a simple questionnaire that will do all those jobs.

Materials

Handout: Feedback to the Facilitator(s)

Plenary/debrief

None required.

Handout: Feedback to the Facilitator(s)

I / We would be very grateful for your feedback on this workshop. Please complete this sheet and return it at the end of the workshop. Thanks!

The three most helpful things I learned at the workshop:

1.

2.

3.

What I liked best about the workshop:

What I would like to have been different/recommendations for future workshops:

Any other comments on the workshop? (please continue overleaf if there is not enough room)

Name (optional): ....

Activity 92
Stop and Notice

Action for Happiness Key
Trying out, Direction

Small groups

Rationale

Research by Matthew Killingworth and Dan Gilbert and Tim Wilson have shown that people are happier living in the present moment than when they are thinking about the past or the future (ref below). Simply 'coming home' to the present more often can increase happiness. You'll notice that there is more to life if you stop and notice – all you have to do is to stop and notice.

The main aim of this activity is to give participants an opportunity to come back to the present moment and become centred.

Materials

None required.

Process/procedure

- Introduce the activity (as above). *In this activity we're going to spend 3 minutes just stopping and noticing. This will give you a chance to focus on the here and now and come back to your centre.*

- Spend the next 3 minutes just noticing. *"What do you notice right now about where you are? What do you notice about your body? What do you notice about your breathing..."*

- Find a partner and share that experience (- a couple of minutes each way).

Plenary /debrief

- How easy was that?
- What did you feel doing that?
- What did you notice that was nice?
- What gets in the way of just stopping and taking 3 minutes each day to just breathe and come back to the here and now and become centred.

Notes including comments and variations

- After this activity you could follow it up with another activity on becoming grounded, balanced or centred.
- This would be a good activity to precede one on savouring and appreciating.

Activity 93
Closing Round – 3 Options

Action for Happiness Key
Emotion, Direction, Appreciating

Individual

Rationale

The sessions within a workshop require a sense of closure and that is even more true of the happiness workshop as a whole. A good way of providing such closure is to give the participants the chance to share the significance of the workshop to them by means of a round.

Materials

Pen and paper, happiness journal or smart phone for note-taking.

Process/procedure

The participants are seated in a circle. Here are three options for closing discussion:

1. How did the workshop measure up?

This first option permits the participants to check out their goals for the workshop with what they actually gained from the experience. Of course, this is only an option if you asked the participants for their personal aims for the workshop at the outset – possibly recorded in their happiness journals. Ask them to spend a minute reviewing their aims for the workshop that they recorded at the beginning and then compare them with what they actually gained.

This round requires each participant (preferably also including you as facilitator) to complete the following stems:
  'My main aim in attending this workshop was ...'
  'What I gained was ... '

Don't engage in, or allow, any debate on the contributions and don't ask for explanations. If someone chooses not to participate in this round don't press them.

2. What did I learn, what will I do?

This second option starts with the participants spending a minute or two thinking of one or two learning points from the workshop that are significant to them and any actions they intend to take as a result of participating in the workshop.

Explain that you will shortly ask for a volunteer to share with the rest of the participants either a significant learning point from the workshop or an action they intend to take as a result. Say that after someone has shared you will proceed in a clockwise direction (or anticlockwise – it doesn't matter which as long as the participants know) around the group to give everyone a chance to share. Let them know that it is 'OK to pass when it comes to your turn if you choose to do so'.

If you have introduced 'happiness journals' as part of your workshop then you can ask participants to bring their journal to this last session and select something from it to share.

On a longer workshop you might want to do two rounds with a round of learning points followed by a round of action points. Be careful, however, about over-playing the rounds format and generating 'round-fatigue' amongst the participants.

3. Appreciate and regret

Explain to the participants that the workshop will close with a round to allow them to express what they appreciate about the workshop and any regrets. Tell them that you will be asking for someone to volunteer 'one regret and one appreciation' about the workshop.

Go sequentially round the room (after specifying whether you'll be going clockwise or anti-clockwise in advance) for contributions from the participants. Add that it's 'OK to pass when it comes to your turn if you choose to do so'.

Ask the participants to spend a minute reflecting on what they regret and what they appreciate about the workshop and let them know its OK to jot down any notes if that is helpful. Then ask for a volunteer to start the process. Don't neglect to include yourself in the round.

Some of the regrets may be negative, such as "I came to the workshop hoping to get more theory input and I regret that we didn't". Often, however, the 'regrets' of participants will be positive reactions to the workshop, such as "I regret that the workshop has come to an end as I've had such a good time and learned so much."

Notes including comments and variations

As an alternative to one minute of individual reflection before the round part of the process, ask the participants to spend three minutes talking to a partner about how the workshop has measured up to their expectations, learning points and intended actions or appreciations/regrets respectively.

Before asking the participants to spend a minute in individual reflection do a review of activities in the workshop to remind them of the experiences they have had at the workshop. Another way of reminding them about the ground covered in the workshop is by conducting a brainstorm on 'What have we done in this workshop – what can you remember?'

Activity 94
Dreams

Action for Happiness Key
Meaning, Direction

Individual, pairs

Rationale

Research suggests that having a purpose and meaning in one's life contributes to happiness. The aim of this activity is to help participants find or articulate their own purpose in life. It will also help them find something larger than themselves that they can commit to, and help them articulate the nature of that commitment. This means there is a transcendent, even spiritual, dimension to this activity.

Materials

None required.

Process/procedure

1. Introduce the activity by referring to Martin Luther King's "I have a dream..." speech...." along the following lines:

In 1963 Martin Luther King had a dream. He spoke of that dream in a speech that is one of the most famous speeches in history. He was speaking on the steps of the Lincoln Memorial as part of the American Emancipation March. Slavery was made illegal in 1865 after the American Civil War by the passing of the 13th Amendment to the US Constitution. In 1963, racial segregation and discrimination was still rife in all aspects of American life. In many states, it was illegal for black children and white children to be educated together or to travel together on the same public transport and in many states black people did not have the right to vote. In 1963 Martin Luther King articulated his dream in a speech. Here is an extract

> *"I have a dream that one day this nation will rise up and live out the true meaning of its creed;*
> *"We hold these truths to be self-evident, that all men are created equal."*
>
> *I have a dream that one day on the red hills of Georgia, the sons of former slaves and the sons of former slave owners will be able to sit down together at the table of brotherhood.*
>
> *I have a dream that one day even the state of Mississippi, a state sweltering with the heat of injustice, sweltering with the heat of oppression, will be transformed into an oasis of freedom and justice.*
>
> *I have a dream that my four little children will one day live in a nation where they will not be judged by the colour of their skin but by the content of their character!"*

50 years later the president of the USA is Afro-American and has been elected for a second term of office.

Dreams can be powerful and articulating those dreams can add to that power.

2. Ask participants to let themselves dream of a better world. What most needs healing in the world today? What would make the biggest difference? What is your dream for a better world? What

difference would you like to see? If you don't have a dream then make one up – just think of anything you'd like see better about the world and think about what that would be like.

3. Ask participants to find a partner, preferably someone they don't know, and then take turns articulating their respective dreams.

Plenary/debrief

Who was moved or inspired by what they heard?

The first step in bringing about a better world is to have a dream, the second step is to articulate it and the third step is to do something about it – no matter how small.

- What is one thing you could do to contribute to the realisation of your dream? ...Over the next year?
- What is one thing you could do to contribute to the realisation of your dream? ...Over the next month?
- What is one thing you could do to contribute to the realisation of your dream? ...Over the next week?
- What is one thing you could do to contribute to the realisation of your dream? ...tomorrow?
- What is one thing you could do to contribute to the realisation of your dream? ...today?

Notes including comments and variations

You could add another stage to this process: when you've heard your partner's dream, suggest three small actions that you think might contribute to the realisation of their dream.

Activity 95
Telling Stories

Action for Happiness Key
Relating, Emotion, Trying out, Direction

Pairs

Rationale

The purpose of this activity is to tap into the creative processes and imaginations of participants. There is a quote from E. M. Foster that goes 'how do I know what I think until I hear what I say?' This activity will give participants a chance to learn from what they say.

Materials

None required.

Process/procedure

1. Introduce the activity by explaining the rationale.

2. Find a partner. Partner one starts to tell a story, as imaginatively as possible, that begins with the words: "So this is what it's like to be truly happy, thought Toby as he closed the door behind him. It had all happened so fast. Only a year ago…"

Feel free to invent whatever plot and whatever additional characters you like based on those opening words. You have 2 minutes for this. Don't think too hard about this or strain to make it plausible. This is a chance to just tell an imaginative story and have fun.

3. Find someone else to be your partner. If you've just been a story teller then find a person who has been a listener because you are now going to change roles so that everyone gets to be a story teller and also a listener.

Plenary/debrief

- Was Toby leaving or entering somewhere?
- What does your story say about what makes Toby happy?
- What does your story tell you about what makes you happy?

Notes including comments and variations

When you are a listener pay close attention and try to be as enthralled as possible by what you hear. This will make it easier for your partner to tell their story.

You may want to spend a few moments at the start with your eyes shut imagining what Toby looks like and the scene in which he finds himself.

You may want to flip-chart what makes Toby happy from a range of the participants.

Activity 96
Happiness Advantage

Action for Happiness Key
Exercise, Giving, Relating, Appreciating

Pairs

Rationale

Shawn Achor, author of *The Happiness Advantage*, identified five activities that increase happiness if practised consistently. This activity is about making a start on them.

Materials

None required.

Process/procedure

Preface: Shawn Achor, author of The Happiness Advantage, found that when people engaged in just one of the following five exercises daily for 21 days they experienced a 24% improvement in life satisfaction:
- Write down three things you are grateful for in the last 24 hours
- Take two minutes each day to write a positive experience you've had in the last 24 hours.
- Meditate for two minutes, focusing on your breath going in and out.
- First thing in the morning write a quick email thanking or praising someone in your support network – a family member, a friend, a former teacher.
- Exercise for 10 minutes each day.

During the morning of a one-day workshop make sure that the first four of these are included so that there is just the exercise activity remaining.

1. Introduce the activity by referring to the information above and inform participants that we have done the first four activities at various points during the morning.

2. Invite the participants to find a partner that they don't know and have lunch with them. The brief for the lunch is to:
- Walk for at least 10 minutes before eating.
- Pay your partner a sincere compliment.
- At the end of the lunch thank your partner for their company over lunch.

Plenary/debrief

None required.

Notes including comments and variations

You might like to add the 'conversational flow' activity (from the book *333 Tips for Living Happier Lives*) as an additional part of the briefing for the lunch-time activity.

Activity 97
Appreciating the Big Things

Action for Happiness Key
Meaning, Appreciating, Trying out, Acceptance

Individual

Rationale

This activity is designed to give participants a chance to clarify what they value most in their lives. It will also help them recognise what they appreciate about what they value, and in doing so, help them develop an 'attitude of gratitude'.

Materials

Pen and paper, happiness journal or smart phone for note-taking.

Process/procedure

1. Start this activity with an introduction along the following lines: It is important to value the little things in life but it is even more important to value the big things. But what is a big thing to one may not be a big thing to another. This activity is about appreciating the things in our lives that we value most.

2. Ask participants to jot down five of the big things they value most in their lives (e.g. your health, a particular friend, all your friends, your relationship with your partner if you have one, your family, your faith, your garden, your imagination, the earth and its environment, your memories, your mind ... whatever are the most important things for you personally).

3. Collect 25 of these on a flip chart (or hi-tech equivalent), to illustrate things that people value most. Invite participants to make any adjustments to their own 'five big things they value most'.

4. Now think of three things you appreciate about each of your five big ones.

5. Find a partner and compare and discuss what you've each come up with.

Plenary/debrief

Can we have some examples of the three things you appreciate? Flip-chart them.
Are there any things that other people have come up with that also apply to you? Examples?

Notes including comments and variations

Variation 1: Instead of using the language of appreciation use the language of gratitude i.e. what three things are you most grateful for about the five things that you value most?

Variation 2: Frame the activity in terms of memories rather than appreciation or gratitude i.e. what three happy memories do you have about the five things that you value most?

Variation 3: Add to the last variation '...and what one happy memory would you like to have about each of the five things you value most?'

Activity 98
Trying something else

Action for Happiness Key
Trying out, Direction

Threes

Rationale

It has been said that 'If you always do what you've always done then you'll always get what you've always got.' And getting happiness is no exception. There are lots of reasons why trying out new things can boost our happiness. Here are a few:
1. It reduces the so-called 'hedonic treadmill' i.e. even things you enjoy tend to yield less happiness with repetition. It seems that variety really is the spice of life.
2. You learn by trying out new things and learning increases happiness in many ways, including promoting feelings of accomplishment, mastery and boosts self-confidence. Knowledge really is power so you'll feel more powerful when you increase your knowledge and that includes your power to be happy.
3. The world is changing at an accelerating pace so *not* learning means a declining ability to cope with the emerging new world ... and not coping is an unhappy state of being.
4. Learning provides more options and some of those options may be happier ones than the ones you currently have.

Materials

Some method of displaying the contributions of the participants (e.g. a flip-chart, flip-chart stand, etc**)**

Process/procedure

- Introduce this activity by talking for a few minutes about how trying new things out contributes to more happiness.
- Form groups of 3 and answer the question, 'What have you learnt or tried out for the first time recently?' (5 minutes).
- Ask each trio to report back 4 things that members of the group have tried out and write these on some form of display, such as a flip-chart, that all the participants can see.
- Brainstorm additional new things that participants could try out over the next week.

Plenary/debrief

- Who feels they are stuck in a rut?
- What stops people trying new things out?
- What new things could you do by the end of a week?
- What new things could you personally do by the end of this workshop?

Activity 99
New Views

Action for Happiness Key
Trying out, Relating, Acceptance

Small groups

Rationale

Identifying and applying our personal strengths make an important contribution to our happiness and we have outlined various activities in this book which support us in that goal. We can also use strengths to help us increase our ability to understand situations or experiences from different points of view, by viewing them through the lens of strengths other than our own, and in doing so strengthen the relationships we have with other people.

Materials

Pen and paper, happiness journal or smart phone for note-taking. A handout per group, each outlining 3-4 scenarios and 3-4 strengths 'lenses' (see below for details).

Process/procedure

1. Explain to the group that this exercise is all about viewing situations through different strengths 'lenses', in order to understand better how strengths influence the way we think and behave. Being able to understand strengths other than our own is an important skill and helps build empathy and connection with others.

2. Divide participants into smaller groups of three or four and give each group a handout.

3. On each handout write different scenarios which should be relevant to the group you are working with. For example, relevant scenarios for a parent might be i) helping your child with homework and ii) talking to a teenager about sex and drugs. Relevant scenarios for siblings with elderly parents might be discussing their care options.

Next to each scenario, write a different VIA strength for each group. Appropriate strengths lenses for the above scenarios might be:

Scenario	Group A	Group B	Group C	Group D
Parent helping a child with homework	Leadership	Curiosity	Creativity	Appreciation of Beauty & Excellence
Parent talking to a teenager about sex and drugs	Prudence	Honesty	Self-regulation	Curiosity
Siblings discussing care options for elderly parents	Honesty	Fairness	Kindness	Social Intelligence

These are the lenses through which the group should answer questions such as:

- What goal(s) might someone with this strength have in this scenario?
- What might their main concern be?
- What questions might they ask?
- What might they do in this situation or how might they behave?

You can add any/substitute other questions which are relevant to the scenario.

Ask groups to spend 10-15 minutes answering the questions as if viewing the scenarios through the strength lens assigned to them. Ask them to make notes for the plenary.

Plenary/debrief

Go through each scenario, inviting comments and observations from each group in turn. Compare and contrast the responses between different strengths lenses.

Encourage participants to notice the range of responses to the same scenario, and ask how they can apply perspective-taking in their own lives to improve their relationships and better appreciate and value other people.

Activity 100
Some Things I Like

Action for Happiness Key
Acceptance, Emotion

Pairs

Rationale

Most people seem to focus on their deficits and the things about themselves that need 'fixing', i.e. what's wrong with them. These tend to be things they don't particularly like about themselves. This activity encourages people to focus on what they do like about themselves i.e. some of their positive qualities or strengths.

The main aim of this activity is to give participants an opportunity to celebrate things they do like about themselves.

Materials

None required.

Process/procedure

Ask the participants to find a partner. Then ask the pairs to each take 4 minutes in turn responding to the following:
1. One <u>talent</u> or <u>skill</u> I like about myself.
2. Two <u>physical</u> attributes I like about myself.
3. Three <u>personality qualities</u> I like about myself.

Emphasize that each comment must be positive – in this activity no negative comments are allowed. *For this activity we're suspending the conventions of false modesty and the social taboos on saying nice things about ourselves.*

Plenary/debrief

- When you heard the brief, how many of you said to your partner 'Would you like to go first?' or words to that effect?
- Did you find this a difficult activity at the start?
- How do you feel about it now?

Notes including comments and variations

Variation: you could start the plenary/debrief by asking people to re-assemble in the full group, so that the pairings are no longer so observable. Then ask participants to call out some of the talents and skills they heard – and list these on a flip-chart or similar. Then do the same for the physical attributes. And then do the same for the positive personality qualities. Finally, ask the participants to record some strengths in their happiness journals.

Activity 101
Simple Massage

Action for Happiness Key
Giving, Relating, Emotion

Pairs

Rationale

It has long been known that the hormone *oxytocin* is released by touch, including shaking hands, hugging, holding hands and massage. Research by Paul Zac (2012) has found that moderate-pressure massage primes the brain to release oxytocin which motivates social interaction even with strangers. It doesn't have to be a full body massage. It can just be a head or a foot massage. Or even just massaging hands.

Touch stimulates oxytocin and oxytocin stimulates trust. Oxytocin makes humans more *humane*. By stimulating care-giving, trust and empathy, oxytocin makes a special contribution to the humanity of humankind. A world of greater trust, care-giving and empathy would be a kinder and warmer place and one with significantly more happiness. And with more oxytocin we tend to feel calmer, less fearful, more generous and more loving.

Touch also stimulates the production of another of the 'happiness hormones', dopamine. In addition, according to research by the *Miami Touch Research Institute*, massage therapy reduced the stress hormone, cortisol (by 31%), and increased the happiness hormone serotonin (by 28%) (Field et al, 2005).

The main aim of this activity is to let participants experience the pleasure of massage and the pleasure of giving and receiving.

Materials

None required.

Process/procedure

1. Ask the participants to find a partner and to sit comfortably opposite each other.

2. Invite the participants to gently massage each others hands simultaneously for 2 minutes using moderate pressure.

3. Ask the participants to let their massage gradually become more and more gentle ... becoming as gentle as they can – for 2 minutes.

4. Then ask one partner to stop moving their hands and allow the other partner to continue to gently massage their hands and note how that feels – for 1 minute.

5. Then the other partner reciprocates - for 1 minute.

6. Ask participants to express their appreciation to their partner in any appropriate way.

Plenary/debrief

- How did it feel to receive a massage?
- How did it feel to give a massage?
- Which felt better the 'moderate pressure' massage or the soft pressure massage?
- How did it feel to express your appreciation?
- How did it feel to be appreciated? How can you get more appreciation in your life?
- How can you get more giving and receiving in your life?
- What did you learn from this experience?

You can let these questions lead into a discussion on relaxation, touch, giving and receiving and/or trust. This can also be an end-of-group activity.

Notes including comments and variations

Some people are reticent about touch but no-one has to participate in every activity. You might like to emphasize this when introducing this activity. It's OK to opt out and just observe.

You might also be careful where, i.e. in what context, you use this activity. It is likely to be fine for a workshop at your local complementary health centre but you may not wish to use it with a group of males in a corporate workshop setting.

Here is a variation in the above process/procedure: when you ask the participants to gradually reduce the pressure of their hand massage you can ask the partners to indicate when the pressure is at their preferred level.

You might like to point out that massages relax both body and mind, reducing stress and thereby cortisol levels and if participants don't have a partner with whom they can swap massages then they can massage some part of their own body - massaging your own scalp and face can be particularly relaxing.

Activity 102
Polishing Diamonds

Action for Happiness Key
Emotion, Appreciating,
Acceptance, Meaning

Individual

Rationale

Some people are very future-orientated and don't spend much time in the past at all. There are other people who spend much time in the past ruminating about, for example, what they should've/ shouldn't have done or what they should've / shouldn't have said. The past is also available, however, as a source of happiness in the present but we need to take time to access past experiences of happiness. Happy memories are always available to use as a resource for happiness when we choose to focus on them. Research on 'savouring' (Bryant et al, 2005, 2007) covers savouring the present, the future by enjoying the fruits of our imagination, and savouring the past by enjoying the fruits of our memories. This activity is about re-experiencing happy times from the past.

Our brain compresses and edits memories, saving key elements of the 'story', because it has limited storage capacity. The brain then 'rewrites' the story every time we recall the memory.
(Gilbert, 2007). This means that when we remember a good experience we have some discretion over the story of that experience – i.e. we can add some imagination to the key elements that have been stored. We can polish the diamond that is our happy experience.

The main aim of this activity is to enable participants to enjoy again happy experiences from the past.

Materials

A sheet of paper for each participant and enough pastels for the participants to share.

Process/procedure

1. Take a few moments to sit quietly, close your eyes, allow your breathing to become a little slower and then deeper and let yourself become centred.

2. Start to recall a happy 'memory', perhaps one that involves a member of your family or maybe a recent holiday or perhaps something further back in time.

3. Reconstruct the whole experience in your mind, from just before it started to the end. Imagine that you've been asked to make a short film of the experience. Recall as much detail about it as you can.

4. Step into it and re-experience it from the inside. What were your surroundings? What were you seeing and hearing? What were you feeling?

5. Allow yourself to smile with pleasure as you recall this positive experience … which should enhance the good feelings even more.

6. Give the participants a sheet of paper each and pastels. Ask them to use the pastels to make a picture of the colours and shapes of their happy memory – in some form that

could be abstract or representational. Let them know that accuracy is unimportant; what is important is to dwell on the memory whilst doodling in colour.

Plenary/debrief

- What were some of your memories?
- Did anyone experience any change in their energy or mood levels as they did this activity?
- What kind of changes in energy or mood?
- This activity comes from a book called 'Celebrating Strengths' by Jenny Fox Eades, where it's called 'Pearls'. Why do you think the author chose that name for it?
- What might you do with the picture to get further value from it after the workshop?

Notes including comments and variations

You could put on some relaxing music while you lead the participants through this activity.

You could omit step 6 and instead just ask each participant to share their happy memory with a partner.

Activity 103
Sharing Happiness

Action for Happiness Key
Relating, Trying out, Direction

Pairs, threes

Rationale

Despite the so-called 'negativity bias' most people are at least fairly happy (Myers & Diener, 1996). On a scale of 1 to 10 most people score above 6. Almost no-one's score is down at 1, so almost everyone has some happiness in their lives. Unless anyone is clinically depressed, it is likely that everyone will be in the 3-8 range, meaning that everyone will have some happiness in their lives they could share.

Maybe there is no simple secret of happiness but rather a large complex secret of happiness and we've each figured out at least a little part of it. This activity provides an opportunity for people to share what they've discovered so far about living a happier life. The aim of this activity is therefore to collect and share what the participants have found out from experience or otherwise about how to be happier.

Materials

Happiness journals, pen and paper or smart phones for note-taking.

Process/procedure

1. Introduce the activity using the words like those in the introduction above.
2. Ask participants to form pairs or 3-somes and each person spend a minute telling their partner(s) what they've learned about becoming happier; something that works for them in living a happier life i.e. something they can recommend about living a happier life.
3. Afterwards, ask participants to call out any particularly valuable or interesting ideas they've heard from their partner/group for increasing happiness and capture these on a flip-chart or similar.

Plenary/debrief

- Which of these ideas sounded most promising?
- Which of the ideas sounded most interesting?
- Which ideas are you going to try out?

Notes including comments and variations

Variation: Use the nominal group technique (see the appendix for a description of this technique) to produce a ranked listing of the ideas for living happier lives.

Another variation is to re-orient the activity towards what participants have found out about *sharing* happiness. In this case the instruction to the participants would be something like: 'tell your partner(s) what you've learned about sharing your happiness/something that works for you in sharing your happiness, i.e. something you can recommend'.

Activity 104
Whose Strengths?

Action for Happiness Key
Relating, Giving, Appreciating, Acceptance

Individual and group

Rationale

This is an activity for a workshop with a group of people who already know each other, possibly as work colleagues. So it would be particularly appropriate in a corporate setting or in a class within a school or college …or even in a family. After this activity participants will know each other's strengths rather better! It can be a great team-building activity.

Materials

Handout: Signature Strengths. Sheet of paper per person. A pen each, all with the same colour ink (to make it more difficult for people to recognise the writing of other participants). A small box.

Process/procedure

1. Introduce the activity by extolling the value of focusing more on our strengths, both individually and within groups.

2. Give each participant a list of strengths from the VIA Classification (Peterson and Seligman, 2004). These are reproduced on the handout below.

3. Ask participants to each decide which 5 strengths they use most and keep their decisions to themselves. Each of the participants then writes their top 5 strengths in capital letters on a sheet of paper without putting their name on it and posts it in the box.

4. Give the box a shake and then empty it out on to the table and participants have to try to match which list of top 5 strengths applies to each of their colleagues. The ensuing discussion will give participants a chance to articulate positive thoughts about each other. It should be strongly supportive.

5. Each participant recovers their own sheet. Encourage them to comment on any other key strengths they have observed in others in addition the 5 identified.

Plenary/debrief

This can be a long activity so there is no real need for a plenary. But if there is time you can ask participants which additional strength (identified by other participants) they were most pleased to receive. Did any observed strength surprise them?

Handout: Signature Strengths

- Creativity
- Curiosity
- Open-mindedness
- Love of learning
- Perspective
- Courage
- Persistence
- Honesty
- Vitality
- Love
- Kindness & Generosity
- Social Intelligence
- Teamwork
- Fairness
- Leadership
- Forgiveness
- Humility & Modesty
- Prudence
- Self-control
- Appreciation of beauty
- Gratitude
- Hope
- Humour
- Spirituality

(© Peterson, C. and Seligman, M. (2004). *Character Strengths and Virtues: A Handbook and Classification*. New York: Oxford University Press.

Notes including comments and variations

Here are a couple of variations:
- If you have a lot of participants in your workshop you can do this activity in groups of 5 or 6 people.
- Instead of asking participants to self-select their top 5 strengths you could ask them to do the VIA strengths assessment (which is available on-line and should take about 15 minutes). There is a short version here: www.viame.org.

Activity 105
What Strengths?

Action for Happiness Key
Relating, Giving, Appreciating, Acceptance

Individual, small groups

Rationale

Like the preceding activity, 'Whose strengths?', this is an activity for a workshop with a group of people who already know each other, possibly as work colleagues. So it would be particularly appropriate in a corporate setting or in a class within a school or college. The main aim of this activity is to help participants develop an awareness of their own strengths and those of their colleagues.

Materials

Handout: Signature Strengths (see activity 104). Online access and time for participants to complete the VIA strengths assessment (approximately 15 minutes each at www.viame.org).

Process/procedure

1. Introduce the activity by emphasising the importance of focusing on our strengths rather than our deficits – for productivity as well as happiness. And stress the value of knowing and using our strengths.

2. Give each participant a list of strengths from the VIA Classification (Peterson and Seligman, 2004). These are reproduced as the handout for the previous activity 104 ('Whose strengths?')

3. Ask participants to each decide which of the strengths they use most.

4. Then ask the participants to do the VIA strengths assessment (www.viame.org).

5. Ask participants to compare their two lists and consider which they feel is most authentic and accurate for them.

6. Ask participants to form groups of 4 or 5 people (preferably with people they know more well rather than less well).

7. Ask each group to then spend about 30-40 minutes discussing the accuracy of the results from the two sources for each person in turn in the light of how they have experienced that person. This discussion will give participants a chance to articulate positive thoughts about each other. It should be strongly supportive. Invite participants to offer up other strengths they've observed in each member of the group in addition to the ones from the 'Signature strengths' list.

Plenary/debrief

How easy did you find discussing strengths? What examples did you discuss of strengths in action? What other strengths did you observe (ones that are not in the VIA framework, for example)?

Activity 106
Parting Gifts

Action for Happiness Key
Relating, Giving,
Emotion, Acceptance

Individual, small groups

Rationale
This activity is a way of closing a happiness workshop. It provides gifts for participants and in addition helps them distil what they have got from the workshop into advice for others (and themselves).

Materials
Paper and pen or pencil for note–taking.

Process/procedure
1. Ask participants to form groups of 4 or 5 with at least some people they have worked with on other activities in the workshop.
2. Explain the basic process: 'As a gift for each member of your group you will let them know:
    i. *What I appreciate about you.*
    ii. *What you have given me in the workshop*
    iii. *A piece of advice for the future.*'

Ask participants to spend a couple of minutes making a note for each person in the group using the headings above. Get them to write the person's name on the paper. You might suggest people tear up a single sheet of paper into 4 – one piece for each person in their group. Wait until people in each group are ready before asking people to distribute their gifts (i.e. the notes). Depending on time, they might read out the notes or simply hand them to the named person. When receiving their gifts from the other members of their group encourage recipients to say nothing but simply acknowledge them. Emphasize that these gifts are not triggers for discussion; if they want to discuss anything they can save that for after the workshop as this is the last activity.

Plenary/debrief
None required.

Notes including comments and variations
You need to set clear time boundaries for this activity to prevent it leading to discussion which could result in the workshop running over – which may lead to some participants leaving to catch planned buses, trains etc.

Appendix 1: Some Flexible Workshop Processes

This appendix contains details of a few workshop processes that can be used in many different contexts and with many different happiness-related topics. We thought it would be useful to put these into an appendix for several reasons. First, so that we did not have to keep repeating ourselves each time we referred to one of these processes in different activities in the book. Second, so that those of you who are already familiar with these processes do not have to keep reading about them. And third, so that we could deal with them reasonably fully, rather than giving just a brief summary.

1. Brainstorming

Brainstorming has long been regarded as an effective way of generating a large number of ideas on any subject or problem, primarily by suspending evaluation or criticism. Recently, there have been some doubts about whether brainstorming really is more effective than asking a group of individuals to generate ideas on their own. However, in the context of a happiness workshop it serves at least three other purposes:
- It provides a way for participants to share ideas
- It offers a vehicle for participant interaction focused on a particular topic.
- Most participants seem to enjoy the process.

The first thing to do in a brainstorm is to phrase a problem or issue in the form of an open question. For example, 'how many different kinds of happiness are there?' or 'how can you share your happiness with other people?' etc. If you're not sure how to best phrase your question for a brainstorm then starting with the word 'how' is usually a good bet.

The next step is to encourage participants to come up with as many ideas as they can, no matter how implausible. You could say something like 'using your wildest imagination think of as many answers as you can to this question.'

Then state the following 'rules of brainstorming':

- No comments, judgment, criticism or evaluation during the brainstorming phase.
- Come up with as many ideas as possible - at this stage we're looking for quantity not quality.
- Feel free to build on other people's ideas.
- The wilder the ideas the better.

The purpose of these rules is to disengage the critical part of the brain which censors what you think and censors even more what you say.

As participants call out their ideas, display each one (using a flipchart, whiteboard, newsprint or whatever medium you prefer). Do this without commenting on the ideas and don't omit ideas you don't rate – this will rightly be perceived as censoring and will encourage the participants to self-censor. Be alert to participants' criticisms of the ideas being put forward; you might need to give a gentle reminder that all ideas are welcome, regardless of how wild they seem at first glance. You can also put forward your own ideas, thus becoming a contributing member of the group.

You'll probably find that the ideas come in 'waves'. As one wave of ideas ends, you can help trigger the next wave by making encouraging comments, repeating the question or using different ways of asking for more ideas.

When you've generated lots of ideas, what you do next really depends on your main purpose for using the brainstorm. You could move on to evaluating the ideas. Or you could use the material generated by the brainstorm to provide examples for some things that you want to say. For example, if you've brainstormed different kinds of happiness then you might use this as a platform for talking about different dimensions on which happiness varies e.g. level of arousal, such as comparing the happiness of serenity with the happiness of exuberance and noting that the ideas put forward can be placed at different points on this spectrum. Or, then again, you might not wish to do anything further with the results of the brainstorm; a brainstorm of different kinds of happiness could simply serve as an orientation and awareness-expanding exercise, and you may just post up the results around the room to provide a happy 'context' for the workshop.

Variations

Instead of brainstorming the answers to a question, you could brainstorm questions. We have found that brainstorming questions can be very productive and it certainly gets the participants thinking about the topic. For example, you might like to do a brainstorm on 'what questions have you (the participants) got about happiness that you are hoping will be answered in this workshop?'

Instead of just allowing participants to call out ideas, i.e. a free-for-all, an alternative procedure is to use 'rounds' (see next process, below) whereby each person in the group contributes an idea or says 'pass'. Or you can combine the two approaches by starting off with a free-for-all and when the flow of ideas becomes thin you could do a quick round to finish.

2. Quick rounds

When all the participants are seated (or not) in a circle then a quick round is when everyone is asked to make a contribution in turn around the circle. Why might you want to use a quick round? Here are a few reasons:
- A quick round can be very useful for changing the mood of a workshop in a short time. It involves speaking in public or having the full attention of the whole group and this tends to focus the participants on the issue in question.
- It can be useful for getting input from all the participants and sharing it.
- It can bring the focus back to the whole group after a period of individual- or group-work, or after a break.

Rounds are very versatile and we have used them at various different times in a workshop:
- At the start of a workshop. For example: 'Please would each person tell us your name, one thing you bring to this workshop and one thing you'd like to take away from it.'
- Checking the agenda for the workshop. For example: 'Please say what you would add or subtract from the aims of this workshop.'
- At the beginning of a new topic in the workshop. For example: 'Please say a little about any experience you already have with this topic.'
- Checking feelings. This can be particularly helpful in a long workshop lasting more than one day. For example, 'Please say one thing you'd like more of in this workshop and one thing you'd like less of.'
- To finish off a session or the whole workshop. For example, 'Please say one thing you've learned today and one thing you intend to do as a result of participating in this workshop.'

Some people find it quite stressful to have to make a contribution in the presence of the whole group and they will worry about what to say rather than listening to the others, so instead you might want to ask for contributions when people are ready. Another way of making it feel a bit safer is by emphasising that anyone can say 'pass' if they do not wish to say something.

Yet another variation is to have a buzz group (see below) discussion before the round so that participants have an opportunity to test out what they might say to the whole group.

Rounds can become a bit tedious if the group is a large one. The larger the group the more important it is to have precise questions and to encourage succinct responses. You may want to think hard about whether to use rounds if the number in the group has more than about 10 participants, because a 'quick round' with a very large group is unlikely to be very quick.

3. Nominal Group Technique (NGT)

This is a versatile process that includes both ideas generation and ideas evaluation in successive stages. The process has a number of uses:
- To enable participants to share ideas and information.
- To establish the strength of support within a group for the different ideas which emerge.
- To avoid the situation where a single individual or subgroup dominates the discussion.

Spend a few minutes introducing the idea of nominal group technique and the reasons for using it.

Here are the steps involved in NGT:

Step 1: *The question*. Identify an open-ended question, such as 'In what ways can an organisation increase the happiness of its employees?' Ask each person to spend a few minutes writing down three to five brief suggestions.

Step 2: *Round-robin recording of ideas*. Go round the group and collect one idea from each person, writing them on the flipchart so that they can all be seen. There is no discussion, explanation or justification of the ideas at this stage. There is no need to reach a consensus either. For example, if there are two contradictory statements they can both be included on the list.

Step 3: *Clarify each idea*. Check that each idea is understood by all the group members.

Step 4: *Voting*. Participants individually evaluate the ideas, giving a 5 for the best or most important, 4 for the idea ranked second, 3 for the next best and so on. Collect in the votes and rank items according to the number of votes secured.

This process probably sounds more complicated than it is. Groups rarely experience any difficulty at all with it.

Variations

A simpler voting method is to give each person five votes to give to the five ideas they regard as best or most important.

Instead of collecting in the votes by the participants calling them out, the participants can be given some coloured sticky dots (e.g. red for first choice, yellow for second choice, blue for third choice and so on).

You could use the NGT process to assess the relative support for each of the aims of the workshop, especially if your workshop has a lot of them, for example if you've added the participants' aims to your own.

You can use the above process for up to about 15 participants. If you have more than that then you can divide the participants into groups. Give each group some flip chart paper, blu-tack and a marker pen. Explain that the rest of the process is a group-based activity and will comprise the following steps (which you may choose to display using a projector, flip chart etc):

Step 1: Group leader. Decide on a group leader to record ideas on the flip chart.

Step 2: Round-robin recording of ideas. The leader goes round the group and collects one idea from each person, writing them on the flip chart so that they can all be seen. There is no discussion, explanation or justification of the ideas at this stage. There is no need to reach a consensus on the ideas. For example, if there are two contradictory statements they can both be included on the list.

Step 3: Clarify each idea. The leader checks that all the group members understand each idea.

Step 4: Voting. Participants individually evaluate the ideas, giving a 5 for the best or most important, 4 for the idea ranked second, 3 for the next best and so on. Then the leader collects in the votes and ranks items according to the number of votes secured.

Step 5: Report back. The leader reports back on the group results.

4. Buzz Groups

A buzz group is a very small group (2 to 4 persons) who discuss an issue for a short period (2 to 10 minutes). Why use buzz groups? Here are the main reasons:
- They can be used to generate energy when the group is wilting.
- They are a way of sharing ideas.
- They are a good way of generating participant interaction, even if you have little control over the layout of the room.

Ask the participants to form small groups of 2, 3 or 4 people by turning to those nearest them to discuss their responses to whatever issue you want them to consider. You might, for example, give them a specific question to answer such as 'What are your happiest memories?' Or you could ask them to discuss 'What ways they have for bouncing back from difficult experiences'. You could ask them to identify any questions they have about happiness in general or about a topic you are about to move on to.

There is no reason why you shouldn't have a buzz group session quite frequently. But if you do then ensure you vary the questions and activities. Participants will get bored if you keep asking them to do something that is too similar.

After a buzz group session you may wish to collect in answers to the question the groups have discussed, especially if it relates to the personal knowledge or experience of the participants. And you might wish to display the answers (e.g. on a flip chart or white board) as a way of sharing the knowledge and experience of the participants.

You can use buzz groups as the basis of a discussion with the larger group as it gives participants the opportunity to develop their thoughts and rehearse their ideas.

Here are some times when buzz groups can be helpful:

- When you want all the participants to have a chance to talk.
- When energy levels are flagging and you want to wake up the participants.
- You want to change the climate in the room.
- You want to move the focus of the workshop on from a previous topic.
- You've forgotten what to do next and you need to find your notes. In this case your trigger question for the buzz-group could be something like: 'What have you learnt so far?'

Warning: Buzz groups are so-named because they generate much noisy 'buzz'. Don't be surprised at the sudden rise in the noise level when you use them. People usually like buzz groups and it can be difficult to quieten them down to listen to you again. So ending a buzz group is not always easy. You might agree your signal that you want participants' attention (such as raising your hand, which participants copy) with them in advance.

Variations

Buzz groups can be used with other processes. For example, if you want to produce a lively discussion on an issue then you can use buzz groups to help participants to develop their opinions first. More generally, buzz groups can help prepare participants for an activity in the larger group, such as a round.

You can form buzz groups of 2 or 3 people for a few minutes then ask each buzz group to join another buzz group to form larger groups to broaden out the discussion. This is called 'snowballing' as the size of each snowball is doubled in size as you move on to the next stage. To prevent repetition of the discussion it usually makes sense to give the larger group a different but related issue to discuss.

Instead of the buzz groups sitting down you can ask people to stand, move around and talk to other participants about an issue. The participants mingle with other participants and this is sometimes called a 'cocktail party'. You can facilitate this by inviting participants to mingle as they would at a cocktail party, i.e. spending only a couple of minutes with another participant before moving on The instruction to the participants might be something like "Now I'd like you to answer the question, 'What have you done recently to make someone else happier?' and I'd like you to do this talking to someone you don't know for a couple of minutes and then moving on and talking to someone else for a couple of minutes. You've got ten minutes to do this, so you should get to talk briefly to four or five other people." This enables participants to interact with each other, share their ideas and vary what they say as their thoughts develop. When the 10 minutes is over you might wish to harvest the results by asking participants to call out 'what ideas people heard for sharing happiness with others?' And a variation on this cocktail party process is to ask the participants to walk around the room until the music stops or you ring a bell. Then they talk to the person standing nearest them until the music starts again or they hear the bell. You can continue this until each of the participants has spoken to about five other people.

5. Line-up

This is a simple process that can be used when:
- You feel the workshop needs something active, for example after a period of sitting down or individual reflection.
- You would like to introduce some more interaction into the workshop.
- You want to mix the participants up in a random way and get them talking to people they probably don't know.

Ask the participants to line up e.g. by birth date, alphabetically, by how far they've travelled to get to the workshop today or even by shoe size. This will cause a degree of chaos at first as participants talk to other participants they don't know and arrange themselves and gradually order will emerge from the chaos. You can use this process for purposes more directly related to the topic of happiness itself. For example, you could ask the participants to line up by how good they think they are at bouncing back from difficult experiences i.e. by how resilient they are. This can also be a useful process to do before forming groups because it mixes up the participants, it can introduce the basis for some bonding (they will have something in common, i.e. their position on whatever is the criteria for the line-up) and the criteria you use may be relevant to the group-based activity you have in mind.

Appendix 2: Outline Plan for a Happiness Workshop

Rationale and Purpose

Over the last few decades our knowledge about how people can live happier lives has been growing rapidly. The knowledge has largely accumulated in the field of study called positive psychology. There have been various attempts to make this knowledge more widely available through books, magazine articles and even television programmes. This workshop offers an additional medium for disseminating some of this knowledge and conveying it in a way that participants can apply to realise more happiness in their own lives and those of people they care about. The overall purpose of the workshop is to help participants to become happier and to share that happiness with others.

A workshop has a particular advantage over other media: it can include an experiential element. This means that it can go further than intellectual discussion; it can make a difference to how participants actually feel. Additionally, this means that it is more likely to motivate new behaviours to realise greater happiness. Simply reading about the findings of studies on the sources and causes of happiness will not in itself increase happiness unless it leads to new actions and changes in behaviour. This happiness workshop is more likely to lead to new actions because it engages not only the intellect but also the emotions and actions.

Aims

The aim is to provide a workshop that will contribute to a happier world. The workshop will do this by:
1. Conveying some knowledge to the participants about how to realise more sustainable happiness.
2. Developing the commitment of participants to take action to increase their own happiness.
3. Providing participants with ideas for what they can do to increase the happiness of those they care about.
4. Directly enhancing the positive feelings of participants so that they leave the workshop happier than when they arrived.

Processes

Most of the processes in this workshop will be drawn from the book '*101 Activities for Happiness Workshops*' and together they will meet the following criteria:

1. Plenty of opportunities for participants to share experience – where they can use each other's experience, knowledge and expertise as a resource.
2. Active learning - where the participants can do things.
3. Variety of processes – to capture and hold their attention.
4. Activities that engage participants' intellects, actions and emotions.

Content

The workshop contains two different types of activities: those which are underpinned by evidence-based knowledge about enhancing happiness and those which are included simply to make the workshop as effective as possible.

Appendix 3: Sample Programme Design for a Happiness Workshop

This workshop is a general one for people who want to know more about the science of happiness and well-being and who want to know how to apply it to lead happier lives. It could also be used as the basis for the first day of a two-day workshop. The overall design strategy is to start off with some high energy activities, particularly in the first session, then shift the focus to knowledge acquisition and before moving on to actions that participants can take to increase their happiness.

Workshop objectives

The objectives of this workshop are to give participants the opportunity to:
1. acquire some evidence-based knowledge about how to live happier lives
2. explore ways of applying what they learn to their own lives
3. discover some ideas about how to share more happiness with those they care about
4. enjoy the workshop
5. meet other people with an interest in living happier lives and sharing that happiness with others.

Summary programme

First session (75 minutes)	*Second session (90 minutes)*
This session starts the workshop. It aims to: • make the participants feel welcome • enable them to meet 2 or 3 other people • identify what the participants want from the workshop • get the workshop off to an active start • convey some knowledge about happiness to the participants.	This is prime time in the workshop. This session aims to: • convey some knowledge about happiness • help the participants discover their own strengths • include activities that participants are likely to enjoy.
Third session (90 minutes)	*Fourth session (90 minutes)*
This is the other prime-time session that can be devoted to conveying knowledge about happiness and taking actions to increase the happiness of self and others. In this session the balance shifts from the former to the latter i.e. from gaining knowledge (which was the main objective of the previous session) to taking actions, in preparation for the fourth and final session of the workshop.	This is the last session of the workshop. It starts with an important theme – happiness in relationships and then goes on to (1) capturing the lessons, (2) turning the lessons into actions, and (3) ending the workshop on a high note.

Detailed Programme with Activities

9.30 First session (75 minutes)	Time (mins)	Cumulative time
Starting the workshop – a warm and welcoming introduction to the workshop	5	5
Participant introductions	10	15
Participant wants and priorities (activity 84)	10	25
A choice of quick activities (50 mins total):		
Finding happiness outside the comfort zone (activity 56), and/or	10	-
Extraordinary achievements (activity 1), and/or	10	-
Reasons to be happy (activity 42), and/or	10	-
42 varieties of happiness (activity 3), and/or	20	-
Some facts about happiness (activity 41)	20	-

10.45 Refreshment break

11.00 Second session (90 minutes)	Time (mins)	Cumulative time
Pub quiz (activity 44)	20	20
What strengths? (activity 105)	50	70
Strengths date (activity 59)	15	85
Giving compliments (activity 10)	5	90

12.30 Lunch

1.15 Third session (90 minutes)	Time (mins)	Cumulative time
Portraits (activity 20)	10	10
Wheel of well-being (activity 68)	25	35
Sharing good news (activity 15)	15	50
Connections and friendship (activity 48)	20	70
Loving kindness meditation (activity 14)	20	90

Other possible activities for this session: Gratitude letter (activity 19)

2.45 Refreshment break

3.00 Fourth session (90 minutes)	Time (mins)	Cumulative time
Support network (activity 4)	20	20
Appreciating our relationships (activity 78)	40	60
Strengths notes (activity 61)	10	70
Closing round – 3 options (activity 93)	10	80
Closing the workshop (a few minutes early) – closing remarks	5	85

4.25 Close

Where to Find Out More about Happiness and Positive Psychology

This section includes a selection of recommended books on happiness and positive psychology, in alphabetical order of author. All are accessible to the lay person, and can be bought for less than £10.

- Ben-Shahar, T. (2007). *Happier*. New York. McGraw-Hill.

- Ben-Shahar, T. (2007). *The pursuit of perfect*. New York. McGraw-Hill.

- Boniwell, I. (2012). *Positive psychology in a nutshell* (2nd Ed). Maidenhead. Open University Press.

- Freeman, D. & Freeman, J. (2012) *You Can Be Happy: The Scientifically Proven Way to Change How you Feel*. London: Pearson.

- Gilbert. D. (2007). *Stumbling on happiness*. London. Harper Perennial.

- Grenville-Cleave. B. (2012). *Positive psychology – A practical guide*. London. Icon Books.

- Grenville-Cleave, B., Boniwell, I. & Tessina, T. (2008). *The happiness equation: 100 factors that can add to or subtract from your happiness*. Avon, MA. Adams Media.

- Haidt, J. (2006). *The happiness hypothesis*. London. Heinemann.

- Layard, R. (2006). *Happiness - Lessons from a new science*. London. Penguin Books.

- Lyubomirsky, S. (2007). *The how of happiness*. London. Sphere.

- Nettle, D. (2006). *Happiness - The science behind your smile*. Oxford. Oxford University Press.

- Seligman, M. (2003). *Authentic happiness*. London. Nicholas Brealey Publishing.

- Seligman, M. (2011). *Flourish*. London. Nicholas Brealey Publishing.

- Style, C. (2011). *Brilliant positive psychology*. Harlow. Pearson Education Ltd.

Useful Websites

www.actionforhappiness.org

Action for Happiness is a movement to create positive social change, launched by the Young Foundation (www.youngfoundation.org) in April 2011. The website contains lots of useful resources such as the 10 Keys to Happier Living and video clips from various scientists and researchers in the field of positive psychology and well-being, as well as postings on what works for them by members of the public. Action for Happiness is free to join.

www.positivepsychology.org

This is the website for the University of Pennsylvania's Positive Psychology Center, directed by Martin Seligman. It's full of useful positive psychology research, information and questionnaires. You do have to register in order to be able to use these questionnaires, but don't worry, this is for academic research purposes only.

www.centreforconfidence.co.uk

The Centre for Confidence and Well-being is a Scottish not-for-profit organisation set up in 2005. The website provides lots of information and research about key positive psychology topics such as happiness, optimism, resilience and mindsets. The Centre's Chief Executive, Carol Craig, writes a regular blog on various topics related to positive psychology including current affairs.

www.ippanetwork.org

This is the website for the International Positive Psychology Association. IPPA's mission is threefold:
- To promote the science of positive psychology and its research-based applications
- To facilitate collaboration among researchers, teachers, students, and practitioners of
- positive psychology around the world and across academic disciplines
- To share the findings of positive psychology with the broadest possible audience.

IPPA's members include researchers, students and practitioners of positive psychology as well as members of the general public who have an interest in the field. Membership benefits include reduced conference fees and access to psychology journals.

www.positivepsychologynews.com

Positive Psychology News is the world's first online journal for news relating to positive psychology. Its authors are primarily graduates of the Universities of Pennsylvania and East London Masters in Applied Positive Psychology programmes, with occasional contributions from guest authors. Topics include coverage of the latest positive psychology research, as well as book and conference reviews, and current affairs. Readers are invited to leave their comments on the articles posted.

www.neweconomics.org

The New Economics Foundation ('economics as if people and the planet mattered') is a UK-based independent 'think-and-do' tank which aims to improve quality of life by challenging mainstream thinking on economic, environmental and social issues. Its National Accounts of Well-being (www.nationalaccountsofwellbeing.org) are oustanding. NEF challenged the traditional GDP-based measures of success and social progress by using comprehensive data from a well-being survey of 22 European nations to construct the first-ever set of national well-being indicators.

www.internationaljournalofwellbeing.org

The International Journal of Well-being is a rare peer-reviewed open access academic journal which was launched in January 2011 to promote interdisciplinary research on well-being. The IJW is sponsored by the Open Polytechnic of New Zealand.

www.uel.ac.uk/programmes/psychology/postgraduate/summary/positivepsychology.htm

This is the website for the University of East London's MSc in Applied Positive Psychology (MAPP) programme, which was the first Masters programme of its kind in Europe, established in 2007.

www.societyandhealth.co.uk/courses/applied-positive-psychology

The Buckinghamshire New University MSc in Applied Positive Psychology, established in 2012.

www.ons.gov.uk/well-being/index.html

The Office for National Statistics' measuring national well-being programme.

www.bangor.ac.uk/mindfulness/research.php.en

The Centre for Mindfulness Research and Practice at the University of Bangor in Wales. Here you can find information about the application of mindfulness in programmes such as mindfulness-based stress reduction (MBSR) and mindfulness-based cognitive therapy (MBCT).

www.workmad.co.uk

On this website you can find further relevant and practical information including:
- Details of Positive Psychology workshops, training, facilitation and consulting.
- A regular blog about applying positive psychology
- Positive psychology resources, books and conferences
- Details of new research findings and updates

References

Achor, S. (2010). *The Happiness Advantage*. London: Random House.
Argyle, M., & Henderson, M. (1984). The rules of friendship. *Journal of social and personal relationships, 1*(2), 211-237.
Bandura, A. (1997). *Self-efficacy: The exercise of control*. New York: Freeman.
Bayer, U. C., Achtziger, A., Gollwitzer, P. M. & Moskowitz, G. (2009). Responding to subliminal cues: Do if-then plans facilitate action preparation and initiation without conscious intent? *Social Cognition, 27,* 183-201.
Bourner, T., O'Hara, S. & Stephens, P. (2014 – forthcoming). *Greater Happiness: 333 Tips for Living Happier Lives*.
Brassai, L., Piko, B. F., & Steger, M. F. (2011). Meaning in life: Is it a protective factor for adolescents' psychological health? *International Journal of Behavioral Medicine, 18,* 44–51.
Breuning, L. (2012). *Meet Your Happy Chemicals*. System/Integrity Press.
Bryant, F., Smart, C. & King, S. (2005). Using the past to enhance the present: Boosting happiness through positive reminiscence. *Journal of Happiness Studies, 6,* 227-260.
Bryant, F. & Veroff, J. (2007). *Savouring: A new model of positive experiences*. Mahwah, NJ: Laurence Erlbaum Associates.
Carney, D.R., Cuddy., A.J.C. & Yap, A.J. (2010). Power posing. *Psychological Science, 21(10),* 1363-1368.
Chamberlain, K., & Zika, S. (1988). Measuring meaning in life: An examination of three scales. *Personality and Individual Differences, 9,* 589–596.
Clifton, D. & Anderson, E. (2001). *StrengthsQuest*. Washington: The Gallup Organization.
Cooperrider, D. & Srivastva, S. (1987) Appreciative inquiry in organizational life. In Woodman, R. W. & Pasmore, W.A. (eds) *Research In Organizational Change And Development,* Vol. 1 (129-169). Stamford, CT: JAI Press.
Damasio, A. (2005) *Descartes' Error: Emotion, Reason, and the Human Brain*, London: Random House.
Davidson, R. with Begley, S. (2012). *The Emotional Life of Your Brain*. London: Hodder and Stoughton.
Davidson, R. J. (2000). Affective style, psychopathology, and resilience: Brain mechanisms and plasticity, *American Psychologist. 55,* 1196-1214.
Davidson, R. J., Kabat-Zinn, J., Schumacher, J., Rosenkranz, M. A., Muller, D., Santorelli, S. F., Urbanowski, F., Harrington, A., Bonus, K., & Sheridan, J. F. (2003). Alterations in brain and immune function produced by mindfulness meditation. *Psychosomatic Medicine, 65,* 564-570.
Debats, D. L., van der Lubbe, P. M., & Wezeman, F. R. A. (1993). On the psychometric properties of the Life Regard Index (LRI): A measure of meaningful life. *Personality and Individual Differences, 14,* 337–345.
Diener, E. (2000). Subjective Wellbeing. *American Psychologist, 55,* 34-43 (2).
Diener, E and Chan M. (2011). Happy People Live Longer: Subjective Well-Being Contributes to Health and Longevity. *Applied Psychology: Health and Well-Being, 3 (1),* 1-43.
Diener, E., Wirtz, D., Tov, W., Kim-Prieto, C., Choi, D., Oishi, S., & Biswas-Diener, R. (2009). New measures of well-being: Flourishing and positive and negative feelings. *Social Indicators Research, 39,* 247-266.
Dunn E., Akin L. & Norton M. (2008). Spending money on others promotes happiness. Science, 319(5870):1687-8.
Dweck, C. (2006). *Mindset: the new psychology of success*. New York: Random House.
Eades, J. (2008). *Celebrating Strengths: Building Strengths-Based Schools*. Coventry: CAPP Press.
Field, T., Hemandez-Reif, M., Diego, M., Schanberg, S. & Kuh, C. (2005). Cortisol decreases and serotonin and dopamine increase following massage therapy. *International Journal of Neuroscience. 115 (10),* 1397-413.
Fowler, J. & Christakis, N. (2010). Cooperative behaviour cascades in human social networks. *Proceedings of the National Academy of Science of the USA, 107(12),* 5334-5338.

Freeman, D. & Freeman, J. (2012). *You Can Be Happy: The Scientifically Proven Way to Change How you Feel.* London: Pearson.
Frankl, V. (2006). *Man's search for meaning*, Boston: Beacon Press.
Frisch, Michael B. (2006). *Quality of Life Therapy: A Life Satisfaction Approach to Positive Psychology and Cognitive Therapy.* Hoboken, New Jersey: Wiley.
Frederickson, B. (2009). *Positivity: Groundbreaking research to release your inner optimist and thrive*, Oxford: Oxford Publications.
Gable, S.L., Reis, H., Impett, E. & Asher, E. (2004). What do you do when things go right? The intrapersonal and interpersonal benefits of sharing positive events. *Journal of Personality and Social Psychology, 87,* 228-245.
Gilbert, D. (2007). *Stumbling on Happiness*, London: Harper Perennial
Gollwitzer, P. M., & Brandstaetter, V. (1997). Implementation intentions and effective goal pursuit. *Journal of Personality and Social Psychology, 73,* 186-199.
Gollwitzer, P. and E. Parks-Stamm (2009). Goal implementation: The benefits and costs of IF-THEN planning. In H. Grant & G. B. Moskowitz (Eds.), *The big book of goals* (pp. 362 - 391). New York: Guilford.
Grenville-Cleave, B. (2012). *Positive Psychology: A Practical Guide.* London: Icon Books.
Grenville-Cleave, B., Boniwell, I. & Tessina, T. (2008). *The Happiness Equation: 100 Factors That Can Add to or Subtract from Your Happiness.* USA: Adams Media.
Haidt, J. (2007). *The Happiness Hypothesis; Putting Ancient Wisdom to the Test of Modern Science.* London: Arrow.
Headey, B., Muffels, R. & Wagner, G. G. (2010). Long-Running German Panel Survey Shows That Personal and Economic Choices, Not Just Genes, Matter for Happiness. *PNAS, 107,* 17922-17926.
Helliwell, J., Layard, R. & Sachs, J. (Eds) (2012). *World Happiness Report*, Columbia University: Earth Institute.
Herzberg, F. (1959). *The motivation to work.* New York: John Wiley and Sons.
Hodges, T. & Clifton, D. (2004). Strengths-based development in practice. In P.A. Linley & S. Joseph (Eds.), *Positive Psychology in Practice* (256–268). New Jersey: Wiley.
Hölzel, B.K. et al. (2011). Mindfulness practice leads to increases in regional brain gray matter density. *Psychiatry Research: Neuroimaging.* 191(1), 36-43) .
Kabat-Zinn, J. (1994). Mindfulness-based interventions in context: Past, present and future. *Clinical Psychology: Science & Practice, 10,* 144-156.
Kabat-Zinn, J. (2006). *Coming to Our Senses: Healing Ourselves and the World Through Mindfulness.* Hyperion
Layard, R. (2011). *Happiness: Lessons from a New Science*, London: Penguin.
Linley, P.A. (2008). *Average to A+.* Coventry: CAPP Press.
Lyubomirsky, S., King, L. & Diener, E (2005) 'The benefits of frequent positive affect: Does happiness lead to success?' *Psychological Bulletin,* 131, pp 803-55.
Lyubomirsky, S (2008). *The How of Happiness: A Practical Guide to Getting The Life You Want.* London: Piatkus.
Lyubomirsky, S. (2013). *The myths of happiness: What should make you happy, but doesn't, what shouldn't make you happy, but does.* New York: Penguin Press.
Killingsworth, M. A. & Gilbert, D. T. (2010). A wandering mind is an unhappy mind. *Science, 330,* 932.
Kubzansky L., Sparrow D., Vokonas P., Kawachi I. (2001). Is the Glass Half Empty or Half Full? A Prospective Study of Optimism and Coronary Heart Disease in the Normative Aging Study. *Psychosomatic Medicine, 63,* 910-916.
McAdams, D. (2008). Personal narratives and the life story. In John, O., Robins, R., & Pervin, L. (Eds.) *Handbook of personality: Theory and research.* (241-261). Guilford Press.
McCullough, M.E. (2001). Forgiveness: Who does it and how do they do it? *Current Directions in Psychological Science, 10,* 194-197.
Medvec, V., Madey, S. & Gilovich, T. (1995). When less is more: Counterfactual thinking and satisfaction among Olympic medallists. *Journal of Personality and Social Psychology.* 69(4), 603-610
Myers. D. & Diener, E. (1996). The pursuit of happiness. *Scientific American, 274,* 54-56.

Myers, D. & Diener, E. (2000). Who is happy? *Scientific American, 274*, 54-56.

Nakamura, J. & Csikszentmihalyi, M. (2010). Effortless attention in everyday life: A systematic phenomenology. In B. Bruya (Ed.), *Effortless attention: A new perspective in the cognitive science of attention and action* (pp. 179-189). Cambridge, MA: MIT Press.

Oswald, A. & Blanchflower, D. (2008). Is well-being U-shaped over the life cycle? Social Science & Medicine, 66(6), 1733-1749.

Otake, K., Shimai, S., Tanaka-Matsumi, J., Otsui, K. & Fredrickson, B.L. (2006). Happy people become happier through kindness: A counting kindnesses intervention. *Journal of Happiness Studies, 7(3)*, 361-375.

Parks-Stamm, E. J., & Gollwitzer, P. M. (2009). Goal implementation: The benefits and costs of IF-THEN planning. In H. Grant & G. B. Moskowitz (Eds.), *The big book of goals* (pp. 362 - 391). New York: Guilford.

Peterson, C. (2006). *A Primer in Positive Psychology*. Oxford: Oxford University Press.

Peterson, C. & Seligman, M. (2004) *Character Strengths and Virtues: A Handbook and Classification*, New York: Oxford University Press.

Rashid, T. (2009). Positive Interventions in Clinical Practice, *Journal of Clinical Psychology, 65*, 461-466.

Rashid, T. & Anjum, A. (2005). *340 ways to use VIA character strengths*. Pennsylvania: University of Pennsylvania (available at http:// www.actionforhappiness.orgmedia/52486/340_ways_to_use_character_strengths .pdf)

Rath, T. (2006). *Vital Friends: The People You Can't Afford to Live Without*, London: Gallup Press

Ricard, M. (2006). *Happiness: a guide to developing life's most important skill*, New York: Little, Brown.

Rilling, J., Gutman, D., Zeh, T., Pagonis, G., Bern's, G. & Kilts, C. (2002). Neural basis of social cooperation. *Neuron, 35*, 395–405.

Ryan R. &Deci, E. (2001) On happiness and human potentials: a review of research on hedonic and eudaimonic well-being. *Annual Review of Psychology, 52*, 142-166.

Schwartz, B. (2004). *The Paradox of Choice*. New York: Harper Collins.

Seligman, M. (2002). *Authentic Happiness: Using the New Positive Psychology to Realize Your Potential for Lasting Fulfillment*. New York: Free Press.

Seligman, M. (2011). *Flourish: A Visionary New Understanding of Happiness and Well-being*. London: Nicholas Brealey Publishing.

Seligman, M., Steen, T.A., Park, N. & Peterson, C. (2005). Positive psychology progress: empirical validation of interventions. *American Psychologist, 60*, 410–421.

Sin, N. & Lyubomirsky, S. (2009). Enhancing well-being and alleviating depressive symptoms with positive psychology interventions: A practice-friendly meta-analysis. *Journal of Clinical Psychology, 65(5)*, 467-487.

Singer, T., Seymour, B., O'Doherty, J., Kaube, H., Dolan, R. & Frith, C. (2004). Empathy for pain involves the affective but not sensory components of pain. *Science. 303(5661)*:1157-62.

Soussignan, R. (2002). Duchenne smile, emotional experience, and autonomic reactivity: a test of the facial feedback hypothesis. *Emotion, 2(1)*, 52.

Steger, M. F., Mann, J., Michels, P., & Cooper, T. (2009). Meaning in life, anxiety, depression, and general health among smoking cessation patients. *Journal of Psychosomatic Research, 67*, 353–358.

Sugawara, S.K., Tanaka, S., Okazaki, S., Watanabe, K. & Sadato, N. (2012). Social rewards enhance offline improvements in motor skill. *PLoS ONE* 7(11): e48174.

Wilson, T. D., & Gilbert, D. T. (2005). Affective forecasting: Knowing what to want. *Current Directions in Psychological Science, 14*, 131-134.

Van Boven, L. & Gilovich, T. (2003). To Do or to Have? That Is the Question. *Journal of Personality and Social Psychology, 85(6)*, 1193-1202.

Veenhoven, R. (2008). Healthy happiness: effects of happiness on physical health and the consequences for preventive health care. *Journal of Happiness Studies*, 9 (3): 449-469

Zac, P. (2012). *The Moral Molecule*, London: Bantam.

Tom Bourner

Until he took early retirement from the university Tom was Head of Research at Brighton Business School and before that he headed up the Management Development Research Unit.

He was also a committed and successful teacher being featured in the *Times Higher Education Supplement's* 'Star Turn' series. Nowadays, Tom's research interests are largely focused on university education, reflective learning, action learning, student-community engagement and ways of identifying talents/strengths.

His other interests include staying fit and healthy, spending time with his wife, Jill, reading (especially works on 'big history', HE, happiness and human development), free-form dance, enjoying the delights of Brighton and otherwise living a simple life. He is a founder-member of the *'Action for Happiness in Brighton'* group and co-author of the book *'Greater Happiness: 333 Tips for Living Happier Lives'*.

Pericles 'Asher' Rospigliosi

Asher Rospigliosi is a principal lecturer in digital marketing, e-business and management information systems at the University of Brighton Business School. His research interests range from Graduate Employability to e-learning and digital innovation in SMEs. Asher has a substantial and successful commercial track record in the development and management of online systems for commerce and education. He recently chaired the first European Conference on Social Media.

Asher's other areas of interest include (in no particular order): Wing Chun Kung Fu, tipis and low impact living, fine dining, reggae music and walking with his two dogs (Cleo and Hermes) on the south downs. He has been firekeeper at the tipi field at Glastonbury Festival for many years.

Bridget Grenville-Cleave

Bridget Grenville-Cleave is the director of Workmad Ltd, which supports both organisations and individuals in improving their performance using applied positive psychology. She is one of a handful of professionals in Europe to have qualified with the MSc in Applied Positive Psychology (MAPP) from the University of East London and is a founder member of the International Positive Psychology Association.

She has written three psychology books including *Positive Psychology - A Practical Guide* (Icon Book, 2012), and *The Happiness Equation* (Adams Media, 2008) co-authored with Dr Ilona Boniwell. She also writes regularly for the global online journal, *Positive Psychology News Daily*.

Bridget runs well-being, resilience and engagement programmes in the health, education and business sectors. She is an accredited trainer for the award-winning Bounce Back Resilience Programme for schools and the Strengthscope assessment for individuals and teams. She is an Associate Lecturer on the UEL MAPP programme and the MSc Business Psychology programme at London Metropolitan University. She regularly gives fun, engaging and practical presentations, talks and workshops on applied positive psychology, happiness and well-being to groups and organisations ranging from the Association of Business Psychologists and the Chartered Institute of Personnel and Development to the local WI.

She has presented research and techniques focussing on the well-being of professional people and communities at Warwick University, the World Congress on Positive Psychology in Philadelphia, USA and the European Conferences on Positive Psychology in Copenhagen and Amsterdam.

Bridget is passionate about community engagement and supports several programmes focussed on improving mental health and developing community strengths and resilience using applied positive psychology.

You can contact her at Bridget@WorkMad.co.uk

Printed in Great Britain
by Amazon